REMEMBERING GRANDMAS' PRECIOUS
Pearls of Wisdom

Remembering Grandmas' Precious
Pearls of Wisdom

DR. CONSTANCE MCMILLAN

Trilogy Christian Publishers

A Wholly Owned Subsidiary of Trinity Broadcasting Network

2442 Michelle Drive

Tustin, CA 92780

Copyright © 2022 by Dr. Constance McMillan

All Scripture quotations, unless otherwise noted, taken from THE HOLY BIBLE, NEW INTERNATIONAL VERSION®, NIV® Copyright © 1973, 1978, 1984, 2011 by Biblica, Inc.® Used by permission. All rights reserved worldwide.

Scripture quotations marked (KJV) taken from The Holy Bible, King James Version. Cambridge Edition: 1769.

All rights reserved, including the right to reproduce this book or portions thereof in any form whatsoever.

For information, address Trilogy Christian Publishing

Rights Department, 2442 Michelle Drive, Tustin, Ca 92780.

Trilogy Christian Publishing/ TBN and colophon are trademarks of Trinity Broadcasting Network.

For information about special discounts for bulk purchases, please contact Trilogy Christian Publishing.

Manufactured in the United States of America

Trilogy Disclaimer: The views and content expressed in this book are those of the author and may not necessarily reflect the views and doctrine of Trilogy Christian Publishing or the Trinity Broadcasting Network.

10 9 8 7 6 5 4 3 2 1

Library of Congress Cataloging-in-Publication Data is available.

ISBN 979-8-88738-077-3

ISBN 979-8-88738-078-0 (ebook)

Contents

Disclaimer 7
Dedication 9
Introduction 11

CHAPTER 1: THE BEGINNING 13
   As a Little Girl 13
      Not Paying Attention 14
      I Have to Share? 15
      Being Falsely Accused 16
      School Integration in 1966 17
      The Challenges of High School at Louisville Academy 20
      Sharing the Negatives of the White School
      with Grandma Maybelle 21
      Not Belonging 24
      The Challenge of Moving to Tenth Grade 24
      Tenth Grade through Graduation Day in 1970 26
      The Incident That Brought About Positive Change for Me 27
      The Prom Dress for My Senior Prom 30
      "Connie, have some shame." 30
      The Graduation Gift 30

**CHAPTER 2: PREPARING FOR LIFE AWAY
FROM MY GRANDMAS** 33
   Becoming an Adult 33
      To Marry or Not to Marry? 35
      Decisions 36
      Attending Dental Technology School in Atlanta, GA 39
      Are You a Maid? 41
      Failing to Follow "My First Mind" 41
      The Unexplained Police Stop 43
   Ms. Jackson Gets a Marriage Proposal
   and a New York Job Offer 44
   Graduation from Dental Technology School
   and Moving Forward with My Life 46

**CHAPTER 3: GRANDMAS' PEARLS OF WISDOM
BECOMING REALITY IN MY LIFE** 49

HAVING CHILDREN 49
    My Out-of-Body Experience 50
    A Baby Girl is Born 51
    What a Difference a Baby Makes! 52
    The Blessing of My Children 54
LIFE IN ALL ITS GLORY 55
    My First Job 55
    Learning That People Will Lie to You without a Care 56
    God's Plan Being the Best Plan 57
GOD STEPS IN WITHOUT MY KNOWLEDGE 60
    Going with My Cousin to Apply for Her "Dream Job" 60
    Life-Changing at the Speed of Light 63
    The Phone Call and the Letter Arrive 64
    Facing Personal Challenges 64
    Graduating as a Flight Attendant 65
    The Real Life of a Flight Attendant 66
    A View of Arrogance versus Humility 67
    Important Memories 68
    Grandma Lula's First Flight 69
    Mom and Dad's First Flight 70
    Jim's First Trip 71
A NEW WORLD OF OPPORTUNITIES 71
    The Conversation That Changed My Direction 73

CHAPTER 4: LOSING MY GRANDMAS 75
    GRANDMA LULA 75
        The Discussion with Grandma Lula after Returning Home 77
        Grandma Lula's Last Ride Home with Sonya and Me 78
        The Phone Call That Changed Everything 79
        Learning to Let Go 80
    GRANDMA MAYBELLE 82
        My Last Time with Grandma Maybelle 83
        A Request That Could Not Be Ignored 84
        Grandma Maybelle Meets Jesus 84
    REMEMBERING THE GOOD TIMES WITH MY GRANDMAS 86

CHAPTER 5: DEALING WITH LIFE'S HARD BLOWS 87
    Betrayal 87
    Growing Apart 88

    The Downward Spiral 89
    Guidance with Godly Advice 90
    The Twenty-Year Mark 91
    Having to Break the News to the Children 91
    Working on ME 92
    Changes within the Airline Industry 93

CHAPTER 6: WHAT NOW? 95
    LIFE IS VIEWED DIFFERENTLY TODAY 95
    What I Was Exposed to as a Child 96
    Raising My Children 97
    THE WISDOM THAT I OFFER AS A GRANDMA 98
    My Sayings 98

Disclaimer

Unless otherwise indicated, names other than the author, the author's children, parents, grandparents, great aunts, and the name of the school are used in a fictitious manner. Any resemblance to actual persons, whether living or dead, or actual events is merely coincidental.

Dedication

This book is dedicated to the beautiful family with whom God blessed me. First, to my parents, Robert Lewis and Elouise Tremble, who taught me to love and always follow my dreams as long as God led me.

To my wonderful husband Mac, who taught me the importance of love and has always loved me without desiring anything other than the love I confess for him and to continue to follow Jesus. To my children Sonya and Karic, who continue to bring me joy with each passing day. To Vimarli, whom God blessed Mac and me to have as our very own daughter—your bright smile and cheerful outlook continually bless us each day. To Tanisha, whose giggle makes us smile, and to our ten beautiful grandchildren we count as angels sent from heaven to love back.

To Dr. Firdina Hyman, who is the reason that this book came into being as my continuous repetition of my grandmas' pearls of wisdom inspired her to tell me to "write a book about those sayings to share with the world." To Terri Smith, who, like Firdina, is a sister who listens patiently over the phone as I talk about the good, the bad, and the horrible without hanging up on me. To Maureen Milliner, who has been my prayer partner and sister for more than twenty years, always loving me and supporting me in prayer.

However, the people to whom this book is forever dedicated are my grandma Maybelle Tremble and grandma Lula Brown, who inspired me until Jesus called them home. They loved the Lord and practiced that love each day of their lives. Their motto was "Jesus first," with everything else following. They were Proverbs 31 women who earned respect from everyone whom they touched.

I look forward to seeing them as well as my beautiful parents in heaven one day!

Introduction

The year 2020 will be remembered in history as the year that brought about COVID-19, a pandemic that stole the lives of millions of people around the world. And while death is finality as far as life on earth is concerned, for millions of others, the pandemic ushered in the loss of jobs and loved ones and the discovery that in a moment, life can change in ways that are unforeseen.

COVID-19 changed our personal lives too, in ways we had never expected. My son, his wonderful wife, and our three grandchildren, then aged eleven, five, and two, lived only thirty minutes away from my husband and me. Our weekly visits had to stop, and before we could make that adjustment, our son informed us that they were moving to North Carolina for some professional opportunities. To say we were heartbroken is an understatement. But we wanted them to do what was best for them and our grandbabies. I began to think about the times I would miss seeing them grow up and how I would adjust to that. Then came the thoughts of my grandmas and how I was so remarkably close to them. My mind became flooded with all the times I had spent with them and how they shared their life stories with me, filled with wisdom. And while these women were ordinary women, they were godly women who read the Bible or had the Bible read to them, attended church, and made it a practice to help others.

So, ladies and gentlemen, here is the product of their wisdom and stories being shared with you! I hope that as you read the story of my life and how the wisdom of my grandmothers came to life, you will come away with an understanding of my grandmas' precious pearls of wisdom. May these sayings bless you with wisdom too. Happy reading!

CHAPTER 1
THE BEGINNING

AS A LITTLE GIRL

Nothing is better than going to Grandma's house. I was incredibly blessed to live with my parents and maternal grandma Lula and visit my paternal grandma Maybelle. Both grandmas lived in the same town, which was a tremendous blessing for me. I was the first grandchild on Mama's side of the family and the first granddaughter on my daddy's side of the family. Life was good! I share the sayings of my grandmas because my paternal grandfather (Fred) died before I was born, and my maternal grandfather (Moses) died when I was six. I remember Grandfather's funeral even today as he died two days before Christmas in 1958. The Christmas wreath on the front door was replaced with a black wreath, and I remember my mother comforting my grandma Lula. It was, at best, challenging for me to understand what death meant. But the memory of that loss prevented me from placing a Christmas wreath on the door of my home until I was sixty years old.

My grandfather also served in the US Army. I remember someone bringing me to the car that we rode to the funeral and seeing the soldiers fire their guns in honor of my grandfather. This was the saddest Christmas in my life with the memory of my mama, daddy, Grandma Lula, and my uncles and aunts crying. Some days later, Grandma Lula told me that my grandfather was with Jesus, which was a good thing. Her reassuring smile as she told me this stayed with me for a long time and made my world perfect again.

When I started school, the world seemed different in a weird way. I learned about brothers and sisters and that I did not have any. I asked my mother what this meant, and she shared that I was special and that while I did not have any brothers or sisters, I still had family that loved me. Of course, I needed to get some advice from both of my grandmas about this.

Grandma Lula said,

> "It was the plan of God for you to be the only child,"

and Grandma Maybelle said,

> "Children come from God, so be thankful for the life you got. Never question what God does or does not do."

All of this sounded good to me and satisfied my inquiry.

Not Paying Attention

By the time I was in third grade, I had found that I liked school and learning. But there were times when I found myself daydreaming or doing anything but paying attention to what the teacher was sharing. If someone was writing a note or coloring in a coloring book, I was totally focused on what they were doing. When I came home and it was time to do my homework, my mother would ask what I learned in school and would review my homework. Since my mother had also been a teacher, there was no way for me to escape answering her questions in detail. But, of course, I could not do that because I did not pay attention. My mother became somewhat disgruntled with my behavior.

One Sunday after church, Grandma Maybelle came home with us for Sunday dinner. I shared with her that I could not understand why my mother was forever asking me questions about school and homework. In response to my statement Grandma Maybelle said:

> "Learn how to listen—it will keep you from making bad mistakes in life."

It is not so much what Grandma said, but *how* she said it. She explained the importance of paying attention to what was being said as that information would be helpful in my life. While I did not understand the "useful in my life" part, I knew I needed to do what Grandma said. So, from the third grade forward, I made a habit of listening and paying attention. Grandma was right as my mama was pleased with me, and there were fewer problems in my little life. Chalk one up for Grandma's help!

THE BEGINNING

I Have to Share?

Being an only child brought with it a privilege. Everything was *mine*, and I loved it. By living in the rural south, people lived at least half a mile apart from each other. Everyone knew everyone else, which was a good thing, especially if someone needed help. A few other children lived near me, but I did not see them very often; however, occasionally, a neighbor might need something and drop in for a visit. If Mr. Joseph needed some vegetables, he would trade us meat for the vegetables and vice versa. Everyone got along and ensured that no one went without anything needed.

My daddy was a truck driver who delivered commodities to different stores. The vendors knew that my dad had a daughter and would give him boxes of treats for me under the pretense that something was missing in the boxes. These treats included candies, pies, cakes, and such. I loved greeting my daddy when he came home from work because I knew there would be treats! He would drive slowly into the yard with my waiting at the bottom of the steps for him to park the rig. Then, I would hear the door slam on the truck and run to meet him. My daddy was six feet tall, but to me, he could touch heaven. He would bend down with his fingers placed tightly together and let me sit in his hands. He would rock me back and forth, and I would laugh because it tickled me to be rocked! Life was *sooooo* good when Daddy came home. On my daddy's last trip home, he had brought two large boxes of treats, including Mary Janes, squirrel nuts, moon pies, chocolate bars, coconut bars, peppermint candy, crème sodas, cokes, and chocolate soda.

Ms. Wright, our neighbor, had come to the house to see if my dad was at home as her husband was going to do some work on their house and knew that my dad knew about construction. Ms. Wright had four children, and the children were with her. My mama told her that my daddy would be home later in the day. I was about to eat some of the Mary Jane candy that Mama had given to me before Ms. Wright arrived. My mama told me to bring out one of the boxes of candy to share with the other children. In my mind, I thought, *What? Why do I need to give them some of my treats? They have a daddy; let him buy them some treats*. I was moving somewhat slowly as I did not want to do this. I retrieved the box and brought it to my mama. She gave the whole box to Ms. Wright, telling her that she knew the children would enjoy the candy. Ms. Wright thanked my mama at least three times and told her children that they could have some of the treats after dinner. She told my mama that she appreciated it as her children had not had any "store-bought" treats for a long time.

I was so, so sad and went to my room. My grandma Lula watched this entire process and came into my room behind me. She asked me why I was so sad. I explained the situation from my point of view. After listening, Grandma Lula said:

"A closed hand can never receive anything—always have an open hand."

This is one of those times when I asked Grandma what the statement meant. She began to tell me that if a person never gives, they can never receive. She said:

"You have lots of treats—those children only have the treats that your mama gave to them. It is better to give than to receive, and I hope you can understand that. Being selfish is not good, and if you don't change and become a giver, life will not be good for you. Selfishness is evil."

Grandma left my room as quickly as she had entered, with my having a lot to think about. Suddenly I was not as sad but felt a little bit of fear because I had learned in Sunday school that evil was bad, and I did not want to do anything that would cause evil to come my way. But in all honesty, I missed those treats!

Being Falsely Accused

Every girl remembers that first boyfriend. It is a special feeling that really cannot be put into words. The boy I liked in eighth grade for a boyfriend was named James; however, he did not know that I existed as he liked another girl named Patrice. I was heartbroken! But there was a boy who liked me whose name was Tyrone. Even though Tyrone was a nice boy, I could not stand him. He moved too slow, constantly pulled on his glasses, and had what I felt to be an irritating voice. Not to mention, he was always bringing me flowers, candy, or something to school every day. I did not want to hurt his feelings, but I also did not want him to bring me stuff daily at school. Finally, I saw that he was alone, and I asked if I could talk to him. He was so excited that I was talking to him; however, he became furious when I told him that he was nice but that I did not want him to bring me flowers or candy or anything else. He walked away from me and told other boys that I was mean to him and that I thought he was not good enough for me. At such a youthful age, it was hard for me to understand why he lied on me.

Now my feelings were hurt, and I decided I never wanted to speak to him again. I knew that I could not talk to my mama or daddy about this, so I waited until Saturday to talk to Grandma Lula. When I shared the story, I cried because Tyrone lied on me to others, and I told my grandma that I would never speak to him again. Grandma Lula said:

> "*It is best to learn how to forgive—not only is it the right thing to do, but it is what God requires.*"

Grandma shared that while this seemed all-important today, I would forget about it in a few years. She shared that:

> "*You have so much to learn, especially in your youth. Never hold grudges and always forgive others so that God will forgive you. Let's replace those tears with a slice of sweet potato pie.*"

Problem solved!

School Integration in 1966

Many things took place in the 1960s relative to civil rights, with the television linking us to the rest of the world. One event that I remember was very upsetting to my mama concerning when the Governor of Alabama, George Wallace, stood at the front door of the University of Alabama to stop two Black students from registering for classes. Mama shared this information with my daddy when he came home from work, with my dad saying he hoped things could change without people dying. The president had to send the National Guard to the school to bring an end to this problem. One name that was continually heard on television was Reverend Martin Luther King Jr., along with commentary emphasizing that he was a preacher who took a stand for all people to be treated equally. Though I was only eleven years of age at the time, I remember four little Black girls being killed at a church with others being hurt. I thought that this was awfully bad since the church was the place for people to come together in love praising the Lord. Grandma Lula and Grandma Maybelle made it clear that there was not to be anything evil happening in God's house as this was a place for profound respect.

There had been talk at church about integration taking place in Louisville. I had not paid attention to the conversation because, for some reason, I did not think that this conversation concerned me—but I could not have been more clueless. Then, one Sunday after church in June, my mama and daddy sat down to talk with me. This was not a good sign. I knew that I had not done anything wrong, but I was just as scared.

My parents informed me that at the beginning of the school year in August, I would attend Louisville Academy, a predominately white school. I thought I had a bad dream. Why would my parents do this to me was the question. I had no problem asking them *why*—humbly, of course. My mother, father, and grandparents highly valued education, so my parents had no problem explaining their decision to me.

Daddy stated that at a meeting of parents and teachers, the school officials chose students to attend the all-white school who were "A" students at the all-Black school. Having met the qualifications, my daddy and mama were asked if they would allow me to attend the all-white school. After spending time thinking about it, my parents felt that this would be an excellent opportunity for me. They also felt that by letting me attend the all-white school, other Black parents would consider allowing their children to attend the school. I knew the decision was final when my father shared that "right now, this is not what you may want to do, but it is your mother's and my responsibility to make sure you have a good education. There are things that are going to be said to you that will be mean and ugly, but we will be here for you." I was in a state of shock! Why was it so vital for me to go to the white school? I was in school already with friends at the Black school. Was going to the Black school not considered to be the right thing for me to do? What mean and ugly things would be said? I had countless questions pouring through my mind, and I did not want to talk to my parents because I felt that they would not understand.

A few days later, my mama and daddy went to pay the bills, and I was at home with my grandma Lula. My escape from anything that I did not like or want to deal with was music. Mama and Daddy bought me a record player with speakers, and my dad bought me the latest music, so I was good to go. Wilson Pickett's "634-5789" sounded good because I truly needed someone to call for help. "Hold on, I'm Comin'" by Sam and Dave was also sounding *really* good about now. I had my bedroom door closed so that I did not disturb my grandma Lula, so I was a little shocked when she knocked on my door and walked in. I cut the music off as she sat on my bed. I sat next to her, not knowing what to expect. She looked at me and smiled and said:

> *"Even when you don't understand why Mama and Daddy do certain things, those things are always for your best. Obey your parents as that is what the Lord requires."*

She explained the importance of education and what it would mean to me later in life. While she explained this importance, I simply listened because of the love and respect I had for her.

My grandma Lula's mother was a teacher, Grandma Lula was a teacher, and my mother was a teacher. My father did not finish high school because his daddy told him that instead of going to school, my daddy needed to work and help take care of the family since he was the oldest child and that he was not going to have a child knowing more than him. My grandma Maybelle did not have a high school education and could not even write. She often talked about marking her X on documents without knowing what the document stated. I will revisit this subject later.

Grandma Lula also reminded me of the importance of staying focused on learning. When she finished talking to me, I did feel better even though I did not understand why I felt better. After all, nothing had changed, but for the moment, I realized that this decision did not come easy for my parents, and I knew that I was in for some significant changes, although I had no idea what those changes would be.

The Challenges of High School at Louisville Academy

Summer was over with the first day of school coming into view. The night before the first day of school, my stomach was in knots, and I do not remember sleeping at all. But sometime that night, I fell asleep as mama woke me up, and I got dressed for school and ate breakfast. Then, I rode the school bus to school. When the bus arrived, teachers were there to meet the bus to ensure that those of us new to the school would not get lost. The first thing that I saw was that everything looked new. The school lockers were shiny, and the books were pristine with no missing pages. Next, a teacher showed me each classroom where I would be attending classes. I can still see the funny looks and the whispering taking place as I walked down the hall with the teacher. Thank God there were a few other Black students at the school with me. Sue and I met in the first class (science) and became good friends. Sue lived near the school, so she walked home, but I had to ride the bus. As I went to my seat on the bus, one boy sitting near the back of the bus hurled the disdainful remark, "Look at (xxxx)..." I was shocked! Who was he talking about? There were feelings of anger and hurt going through me—feelings I had never felt before. I did not know what to do. Finally, the bus driver told the boy (John) that he would be taken off of the bus if he said another word.

When I got home, I ran to my room and cried. My mama came in and asked me what was wrong. I shared with her what had happened. Mama said that she was so sorry that I had that experience, but that was what Black people sometimes experienced when being around white people. My mama talked to me about understanding who I was and not being moved by what people were saying. I was so glad to see Friday come so that I would have two days away from such mean and ugly people saying such mean and ugly things. What good could come out of this situation?

Sharing the Negatives of the White School with Grandma Maybelle

On Saturday, I went to see my grandma Maybelle since my daddy and his brother were going fishing. I shared with her my school experience as well as my disappointment, and she smiled at me in a very loving way. However, she also told me that it was time to face some hard truths with her saying:

> "Disappointment is part of life, so get used to it."

and

> "There are two things to always remember about white people. They will work you like a workhorse mule, and you can't tell 'em nothing. Once you know this, life becomes easier for you!"

Grandma needed a few items to cook her favorite pound cake and decided to walk to the store instead of my driving her there. So, of course, I walked with her, and we were laughing and talking about everything, from when she met Granddaddy to her wanting to go back to school. We met Ms. Jonner, a white woman whom my grandma baked pies or cakes for whenever Ms. Jonner had visitors. About five weeks earlier, Ms. Jonner had asked Grandma to bake some sweet potato pies for her, but Grandma was going to Florida to visit family the following day. Grandma told Ms. Jonner what she did when baking the pies, telling her that since she (Grandma) did not use a written recipe, the pies may be slightly different, but the pies would still be good if she followed what Grandma told her. Ms. Jonner baked the pies but was quite disappointed in how the pies turned out. This was the discussion between Grandma Maybelle and Ms. Jonner:

Ms. Jonner: Lord Maybelle, you messed me up with your recipe for the sweet potato pies. They were horrible, and no one liked them.

Grandma Maybelle: Did you use three medium sweet potatoes?

Ms. Jonner: Yes, I used three sweet potatoes.

Grandma Maybelle: Did you use three sticks of real butter?

Ms. Jonner: Well, no, I used a stick of margarine because I did not have any real butter at the time, and I did not want to go to the store.

Grandma Maybelle: Did you use one egg per pie and add one extra egg and beat the eggs before putting them into the pie mixture?

Ms. Jonner: No, I just used two eggs because I did not think I needed to use that many eggs.

Grandma Maybelle: Did you use one teaspoon of allspice and a three-quarter cup of sugar per pie?

Ms. Jonner: Well, Maybelle, I can't remember. The pies just were not good.

Grandma Maybelle: Well, maybe you will have better luck next time.

As we walked further away, Grandma Maybelle looked at me with a funny smile and said:

> "See what I told you about not being able to tell white folks nothin. I told her how to make the pies, she did not do what I said, but it is MY fault that the pies were bad. I can only imagine what they looked and tasted like."

I laughed not only at what she said, but at the raised eyebrows she used to stress her point. I knew she was serious, and since I was now surrounded by white people five days a week, I was all ears. She shared that as a Black girl, I needed to know my worth and not allow anyone, especially white people, to affect me emotionally. She shared with me her experience in having to work in the fields picking cotton, peaches, pears, and cleaning up white people's homes to make money to take care of the family. So, while I was being called ugly names, I had the opportunity to gain experience about white people and how they acted and reacted. Knowing this was just as important as book learning. Grandma was very firm in what she was saying. She also told me that while there are good people of every race and color, the white man will tend to see you as black, thereby being inferior to him or her. Grandma said:

> "There are bad white people just like there are bad of every people... but what you have to remember is that it is the white folks who are in charge on the job, own the stores where Black folks shop, and are in the big positions making decisions that affect how Black folks live. Never forget that you are Black and that there are people who hate you because you are Black. There ain't nothing that you can do about it but trust King Jesus. If Black folks didn't have Jesus, we wouldn't have nothin'."

Grandma made her point with a splendid example that I witnessed. I wondered if this was the reason, she wanted to walk to the store versus riding to give us extra time to talk. Of all the conversations that I had with Grandma Maybelle, this one has stayed with me all my life, and I was glad we shared that Saturday!

My daddy added something to this scenario as he sat me down on Sunday afternoon to talk with me about my first few days of school. I shared the same story of what had happened to me, expecting my father to hug me and tell me everything would be fine. Instead, my father asked me what the offensive remark meant. I told him that the meaning was not good since a white boy called me by that name. My dad told me to get the dictionary and look up the meaning of the word. The definition of the word meant to be "in derision or depreciation, ignorant." My daddy looked at me and asked if I saw myself as ignorant. I answered, "No." Then my dad told me to stop allowing people to control my emotions and feelings. This conversation ended that day about the offensive remark.

When I arrived at school the next day, it took about ten minutes to realize that the teachings at Louisville Academy exceeded what I had been taught at the Black school at least twenty to one, especially the subjects of science, mathematics, and writing. The science teacher, Mr. Samson, taught the science class from his freshman college notebook. If you did not pay attention in class or failed to take good notes, it was almost next to impossible to pass the tests. On the first day of class Ms. Whitley, our math teacher, wrote a problem on the board, *2(x + 8y)*, and asked one of the students to simplify the expression. I had no idea what she was talking about. I knew I was in trouble.

My following day at school involved homework assignments for each class, including science, math, English, and writing. Looking back, it seemed there were not enough hours in a day to complete my homework. The entire school year involved coming home from school, eating dinner, and working on homework from 4:30 p.m. until at least 11:00 p.m. My parents also informed me that I would not have to do any chores until Saturday morning. Daddy explained that he could not help me with any homework because he did not understand what I was being taught in school. Mama could help me with all my homework but acted as yet another teacher showing me how to find the answers. At first, this was so frustrating, until when I went to bed at night, I would cry myself to sleep. But I had to learn what was being taught because this was the expectation of my parents and grandparents. To fail meant not only failure for me but disappointment for my family.

Not Belonging

By attending Louisville Academy, it was as though I did not belong anywhere. Friends that I thought I had when attending Jefferson County School no longer saw me as black but as a Black person who thought I was white. The students at Louisville Academy saw me as insignificant and ignorant, having no problem calling me out of my name. It was as though I did not fit in anywhere. But the good thing was that my parents and grandmas still loved me, so I knew that I would make it. The situation made me desire to succeed even more as the Black kids had stated that I would not graduate in 1970 because the white people would make sure that I failed. I had to make it, as there was no other choice.

The Challenge of Moving to Tenth Grade

I needed to pass four units to move to tenth grade. I finished the math, English, and writing classes with B's; however, I finished the science class with a 69.5-grade average needing a 70-grade average. Mr. Samson let me know that he did not believe in rounding grades up. What he should have said was he did not round grades up for the

Black students. This meant that for me to advance to the tenth grade, I needed to go to summer school and re-take the science class.

My mother had been a teacher for several years before and after marrying my dad. After I was born, she enjoyed being at home with me as they lived in Augusta, GA. When her dad became ill, my mama and daddy moved back to Louisville to help my grandma Lula. This was also a challenging time for them as my daddy had been told by his uncle that if he moved to Detroit, MI, my dad could get a job with General Motors. The money would have been at least three times what he was making driving trucks with my daddy's uncle also having a place for my daddy to stay until he could find a home for my mama and me. After Granddaddy Moses died, Mama did not want to leave Grandma Lula alone, and Grandma did not want to leave the home she had shared with Granddaddy for more than forty years. Later in my life, my daddy shared that he wondered how different our lives might have been if he could have taken advantage of that opportunity. I asked my dad if he had regrets about it, and he said "*no*" because life's perfect order was God and family. He knew he had made the right decision to stay in Louisville with my mama, me, and Grandma Lula. That was the end of that conversation, and it was never mentioned again.

My mama had thought about returning to work after Granddaddy died; however, my dad wanted her to be at home when I came home from school. But once I was in high school, my mother decided to go to work to ensure that I could have anything I needed or wanted while attending high school. My daddy agreed with my mother, taking a position at the manufacturing plant where my dad worked as a machinist. Teaching had changed since my mother had taught school, and she felt that she could earn a better income working at the plant.

It would take $90 for me to go to summer school, as well as my parents paying Ms. Wright $15 a week to take me to school in the mornings. In 1966–67 this was a nice chunk of change, but my parents made it happen. Rather than taking only one course, I also took an additional course in mathematics to ensure I was ahead of the class. I passed both courses in summer school and made it to tenth grade on schedule.

Tenth Grade through Graduation Day in 1970

Beginning tenth grade was somewhat easier because now I knew what to expect. There were still a few name-callers at the school, but a change was taking place. Some white students began to talk to me, telling me what their parents had said about Black people. Now that they were going to school with us, they realized that what was said was not true. So, of course, I asked what their parents had said about Black people. One girl shared that her parents never talked about Black people but that her grandparents had said that Black people were lazy and lived by stealing. Another girl said that her dad did not like Black people because they always tried to beat white people out of something. Another girl said that her parents did not spend too much time with her grandparents because of their prejudice and not liking Black people or Jews. My classmates' grandparents also felt that by Black kids going to the white school, the next thing would be white boys marrying Black girls, thereby polluting the white race. My first thought was how sad for people to make assumptions that have never been proven.

I became friends with a girl whose name was Lorna. She was different from many other white girls because she did not try to fit in with the other girls. I also met Marcia, and the three of us became friends. There was another girl whose name was Lynn. She was seen as an outsider because her family was classified as "poor whites." I spent a lot of time with Lynn because I liked her, and I understood how she was treated. When Lynn and I were together, I also noticed that Lorna would just stay away. Finally, one day after school, I talked to Lorna to let her know that I liked Lynn and that if she took the time to know Lynn, she would like her also. It took some time, but eventually, Lorna would sit with Lynn and me at lunch, with Sue joining us sometimes. Later that year, I met Nicki with these four girls sharing that they realized that the only difference between them and me was my skin color. This was a learning experience for each of us, discovering that people should not be pre-judged based on what others think and say, instead, decisions about people should be made based on one's own interactions and experiences.

THE BEGINNING

The Incident That Brought About Positive Change for Me

One day at school, I ran late getting to math class because I had stayed to ask a question in my English class. As I was running through the classroom door, I heard a voice behind the door identifying me with a derisive ethnic slur. I lost it and came around the door and began to hit the two boys sitting behind the door (Jeremy and Craig) with my books, compass, and purse. I was hitting them, crying, and shouting at the top of my voice, "I'm tired of being called out of my name by you because I am a Black girl, and I am not taking this anymore." This incident probably lasted at most a minute; however, it seemed like hours to me. Suddenly, I came back into reality and realized what I was doing. I knew that my parents would kill me (parents ruled when I was a child with dialing 911 not being an option. We had rotary phones back then where you dialed one number at a time). I knew that Ms. Whitley would walk me to the principal's office with the principal calling my parents. When I stopped hitting the two boys, classmates were helping me pick up my things, and Ms. Whitley said, "Class, turn to page 261." That was the last time a hurtful racial slur was used to describe me at Louisville Academy, and I did not share this story with my parents until I was an adult, although I am quite sure they heard about it at work from the boys' parents.

As we approached the end of the school year in 1968, an event occurred that changed the world. Dr. Martin Luther King, Jr. was assassinated on a hotel balcony where he was staying in Memphis, TN. His death brought such sadness to the world, with some in the Black community blaming all white people for what one man had done.

A special service was called at the church with my parents, grandparents, and me attending. The service concerned special prayer for the King family as well as the world after the assassination of Reverend Martin L. King, Jr. My parents talked to me about the event to see if I really understood. I told them that I did and that I was sad for the Black community but sadder because Dr. King had a wife and children who had to live without their husband and father. Just the thought of my dad being dead caused my eyes to tear. But they knew that I understood and told me that if I had any questions, I could talk to them at any time.

Returning to school the following Monday was weird. Everyone was simply quiet without the usual chatter that took place when we changed classes. Our history teacher, Ms. Strong, taught the class concerning the assassination allowing us to discuss what we felt Dr. King's death meant to the US. I was pretty surprised at some of the comments from the white students as they made positive comments including Dr. King being a man of peace as well as a preacher. For someone to take his life for what he believed was unacceptable. For the first time since attending the school, I saw people having feelings for someone based on what they were doing versus their color. This was a good feeling flowing inside of me.

The following week Ms. Strong informed us that President Johnson had signed the Civil Rights Act of 1968, which would allow equal housing opportunities for all people without regard for religion or race.

By eleventh grade, I was now making A's and B's and building up self-confidence. I was not moved by what others thought of me but driven by what I thought of myself. The Junior-Senior Prom was incredible, with everyone getting along. By twelfth grade, we were visiting each other's homes, going on a few hayrides together, and just enjoying each other. On the night of the Junior-Senior Prom, the parents had made plans for all the seniors that involved a cookout after the prom and students going to each other's houses to hang out. My mom bought me navy blue and white polka dot pants with a white high-top pullover to wear on the hayride and cookout. My friends also came to my house along with a few of the boys, including Jeremy, the boy who hurled the racial epithet in math class two years earlier. This was the first time I did not need to be home by 11 p.m. because all seniors' parents participated in this celebration. I still treasure the memories of this night.

While I was excited about leaving home, I realized that this was a much bigger step than I had imagined. I talked with Grandma Maybelle about some of my fears, and as always, she had some excellent advice. I asked her if she had ever been somewhere and did not know what to do. She smiled and said that this was something that had occurred to her many times. So, I asked her what she did. Grandma said:

> "When in a place and you don't know what to do, find someone who looks like they know what to do and follow them—but be careful."

She reminded me that it was always important to be open to learning and realize that even a small child could teach an adult something if they were willing to learn. She also said that:

> "Book learning is needed but you must learn from life lessons. Do your best to do what's right, especially when you know what is right."

As graduation moved closer, my parents began to remind me of the simple things that I had practiced all my life. It was important, to be honest, truthful, and to always respect others. Most importantly, I should never forget what I had been taught by my parents, grandparents, uncles, and aunts. These people had experienced many things in life and had shared much knowledge with me over the years that could help me to avoid making the mistakes they had made. It was time to decide about going to college, the type of career I wanted to follow, and things like this. I also talked with my grandma Lula, who shared:

> "Know the difference between making a choice and making a mistake."

I asked Grandma to explain this to me, and she said:

> "A mistake is something that occurred because of a lack of knowledge. You thought that you were buying nutmeg, but because of being in a hurry, you did not discover that someone had placed allspice on the nutmeg spice shelf. That was a mistake. When you choose to drive 70 mph in a 55-mph zone, that was a choice. And do not be surprised if you get a speeding ticket that costs money that you do not have at the moment."

I understood what she was saying.

The Prom Dress for My Senior Prom

I do not remember who was the most excited about the choice of my prom dress, my mama or me. Both of my grandmothers accompanied my mother and me to shop for the dress, which made it even more exciting for me. I looked at one dress that was considered inappropriate by my grandma Maybelle. As I looked at the dress, Grandma Maybelle said:

"Connie, have some shame."

To myself, I thought, *What does that mean?* As we walked to the next store, I asked my mama about this saying. My mother explained that a woman needs to dress appropriately by not showing too much of her body. A woman can dress sexy without being naked. I did not think that any dress we looked at showed nakedness, but I went along with the program. I chose a gorgeous pink taffeta V-necked maxi dress with long pleated sleeves. The dress was out-of-sight as far as I was concerned, and to me, I looked like at least $1 million, maybe $2 million! My grandmothers and my mother liked the dress too, so all was well on that Saturday. My mama dropped $90 for the dress and $30 for the silver shoes and was excited to do it!

The Graduation Gift

As I have previously stated, being an only child was a good thing, especially when getting gifts. I received a gift from a relative that made no sense to me at the time. When my mama gave me the gift, I opened it. The gift looked like a bookmark. I was unsure what to say, so I just set the gift aside. I went to see my grandma Maybelle on Saturday and told her about the gift. She shared with me that:

> "Nobody has to do nothin' for you or give you anything. If someone brings you a glass of water, be thankful cause they didn't have to do it."

This was a particularly important saying to her because one became thirsty working in the fields. Someone taking the time to bring a glass of water to someone else meant so much. I went back home and wrote a beautiful thank-you note appreciating the fact that I was remembered by someone who thought enough of me to send me a gift!

Graduation day came, and it was one of the happiest days of my life. I finished high school at the white school and received an award in the name of a physician who had attended the school in the past. When my Black friends found out that I was attending the white school, they had no problem telling me that I would not graduate in 1970 because the white people would not let me graduate on time. I graduated on May 28, 1970, with the Black high school graduation not occurring until sometime in June. Another memorable moment is that we were the last class to graduate from Louisville Academy as the school was closed so that all the white and Black students could go to the Black school, which was the larger school (go figure)!

But I received some even better news from my grandma Maybelle. I went by to see her on Saturday as usual. When I walked in, she was excited and told me to sit down as she had something to share. I did just that, and to my surprise, she sat down next to me with her Bible. She opened it to Psalms 23 and began to read it to me. I was in shock as Grandma was reading the scripture from the Bible, not reciting it. She looked up at me with tears in her eyes, and all I could do was hug her so tight. She also had a piece of paper in the Bible, and she wrote her name on that paper. I jumped up and said, "Grandma, you can write!" She said "yes." She took classes in reading and writing at the high school that was not too far away from her house. She had been walking to the afternoon classes for six months! She also told me, "Now I can write my name and read! No more marking my X! Don't forget that having an education is important so that you can stand up for yourself!" I was so proud of her! We had our celebratory meal consisting of collard greens, fried chicken, homemade potato salad, cornbread, and sweet potato pie. Believe me when I tell you the meal was delicious and the time spent with my grandma Maybelle was one of the best times ever.

CHAPTER 2
PREPARING FOR LIFE AWAY FROM MY GRANDMAS

BECOMING AN ADULT

All my life had been surrounded by my parents, grandparents, aunts, and uncles. Being the typical teenager approaching graduation from high school, my first thought was to move away from Louisville as quickly as possible. I had watched enough television and saw places that I knew had to be more interesting than Louisville, so I was ready to make a move. My parents took me to Florida to visit relatives and other family members in Savannah, GA; Brunswick, GA; and Detroit, MI. My grandma Lula took me on a train to visit her sister in Detroit when I was about eight. I remember the excitement of being on the train and seeing unusual places as we rode by. It was that excitement that I believed would be happening in my life after leaving Louisville.

At sixteen, I was allowed to have a boyfriend (Jim) who could come by to see me on Sunday. He arrived at 8 p.m., and the knock on the wall by my grandma Lula meant that it was 10 p.m. and he had to go. While most of my friends were making plans to attend college or technical school, I dreamed of becoming an actress like Diahann Carroll or Gail Fisher. It was so nice to see Black women playing roles that did not involve them doing housework. I had not figured out how I would get to Hollywood, but I knew I would get there one day.

But something happened during the summer after I finished high school that changed my plan. My boyfriend started talking about marriage. This was something that I knew I wanted to do because of seeing the happiness shared by my mama and daddy and listening to my grandma Lula talk about the life she shared with my grandpa Moses. So, after the usual Sunday family dinner, I drove Grandma Maybelle home and, along the way, began to talk to her about my plans. She listened intently, and I decided to stay for a while when we got to her house. Grandma began to talk to me differently, as if she were looking right through me. She encouraged me to think about each decision as my life was taking on a different meaning. She said:

> "You are now growing into a grown person who will have to make many decisions. Spend time every day with God—you will find it to be time well spent, and whatever you do, do not make life-changing decisions without hearing from King Jesus."

I asked her: "Is this what you did, Grandma, when you were my age?" Grandma smiled and said:

> "I wish I could have been where you are at your age. But I didn't get a chance to go to school as I worked to help my mama. When I met your grandpa, we got married and soon started a family. I am not talking about regrets but the way the hand of life was dealt to me. I want you to have far better. Keep in mind that no matter what comes your way, time spent with family is time well spent and that at the end of the day, family is what is important. Place nothing before God and family."

Grandma Maybelle was also honest about how she felt about Jim. She said:

> "Remember, baby; the chip don't fly far from the block."

Jim did not talk about his father that much, but one of the disadvantages of living in a small town is that people talk about everybody with total emphasis on the bad. Though Jim's dad had died many years ago, people said that he was a man who loved women and spent more time with other women than his wife. I knew that my grandma knew this, but I asked her, "Didn't you tell me that people can change even when they have made mistakes?" Grandma Maybelle said:

> "That is true, but a person has to want to change in order to make a lasting change. Right now, you are in love, and love can be blind. So, I am going to pray for you and ask God to help you with this marriage thing."

We spent the rest of the time talking about much of nothing as well as my grandma telling me stories from the past that she had shared with me and her other grandchildren at least a thousand times. But you know what? I enjoyed those stories and treasured the time I was spending with her! This was something that I was going to miss when I left home.

To Marry or Not to Marry?

Jim had asked me to marry him, and there was no way that I was going to make this move without the permission and blessing of my parents. When I sat down to share this news with my parents, there was silence. My daddy said he and Mama would like to think about it first. This was the usual as there was never a quick answer from either of my parents about anything. I thanked them and started listening to my music. A few days later, my parents called me to the kitchen table, and we discussed this issue. My parents simply asked me to go to school for at least one year before getting married. If Jim and I loved each other, things would work out. I agreed.

Of course, I had to hear Grandma Lula's opinion on the matter. When I asked her, the answer was short and simple as she said:

> "Marriage brings with it many troubles—spend time in prayer and make sure you hear from God before doing it."

I asked her if that was what she did before marrying Grandpa Moses. She smiled, and through her facial expression, I could see the love that was still in her heart for him even though he had passed away almost twelve years ago. She said:

> "Gal, that is a good question. I think I did, but that was so long ago that I have forgotten. I do remember this. Your grandpa and I prayed together every day and trusted God. When the hard times came, God and our love supported us, and in the good times, God and our love sustained us. I want the same for you."

Grandma Lula was not a big hugger, but at this moment, she hugged me so tight. I always knew that she loved me, but I can still feel that hug. She told me she would miss me but that she was so enormously proud of me. I am sure you can see me beaming from ear to ear even as you are reading this. There is no love like Grandma's love—YES!

Decisions

I talked with Jim about what my parents had asked me to do concerning marriage, with his agreeing. So now I would attend school for at least one year. Several schools had written to me with my not responding to any of them. Ultimately, I responded to all of them and decided to attend the first school that contacted me, a dental technology school in Atlanta, GA. I decided to go to this school as the program was for one year, with classes starting in September. This allowed me to celebrate my eighteenth birthday with my family and start classes the following week.

Jim lived with his sister in Atlanta while looking for a job, and we were also able to see each other. He took the position of machinist at a fabric plant. The pay was excellent, and he liked the work. Jim was an excellent mechanic and could work on anything from cars to machines.

The Dental Technology School had a unique program for students coming to Atlanta from out of town. Some people would allow the students to live in their homes while attending school. Most of these adults had children with the plan for the student to help them with babysitting at least one day a week if needed. The students were also paid an allowance by the parents, being seen as a win-win for everyone. A representative from the school came to our home and talked with my parents and me. My parents liked the idea since there would be someone looking out for me, and I would not be alone. I was to live with a family where the husband traveled extensively, and the wife was a stay-at-home mom with two children, ages three and four. I liked this idea as I had not had the opportunity to live with any smaller children. While my mother's sister's children lived with us off and on for many years, they always ended up going back to Atlanta, GA, at some point until they were twelve, eight, and six years of age. At this point, they lived with us most of the time.

About two weeks before I was to start classes, the family I was to live with notified the school that the husband had been offered an overseas position and the entire family would be moving. I wondered if I had made an unwise decision; however, within two days, the school notified my parents that they had found another family with whom I would live. The woman was a model having a twelve-year-old daughter. My parents liked this idea even better, and so did I.

On a Sunday morning, my mama, daddy, and I left for Atlanta, GA. As we left the house, my grandma Lula waved with tears in her eyes as we drove out of the driveway. The night before my leaving, she shared the sayings:

> "Place nothing in life before God."
>
> "Do not be at people's mercy."
>
> "Don't practice being lazy—nothing good comes of it."
>
> "You will reap what you sow, so be careful of what you do as it will come back to you."
>
> "No matter what people may say when the Lord does something special for you and you KNOW it was the Lord, no one can ever make you deny Jesus!"
>
> "Live life to the fullest so that you will not have a list of regrets when you get old."

Grandma Lula also said that while I may not understand the meaning of these words at the moment, these words would make better sense in days to come. She said:

> "You will have challenges in life that will let you create your own story to share with your grandkids."

I had talked with Grandma Maybelle the day before leaving with her reminding me of every saying she had ever shared in the past while also saying:

> "Never go against your first mind—it is almost always the right choice."
>
> "Some people ain't goin' change no matter how old they git."

"Some people ain't never satisfied. If you got the job for them, worked the job, and bring them the paycheck, they want you to go to the bank and cash the check."

"Keep the 'O' out of your life" (O meaning owe).

"Always show respect for people."

"Know that you preach your funeral every day that you live, and nothing said at the funeral will change that."

"You don't break bread with everybody."

We arrived at Ms. Jackson's home at noon on Sunday. She was a tall, slender white woman with a smile that was warm and open. Her daughter, Nancy, was pretty and had the same manners as I did, saying "please," "thank you," and other niceties that make a child lovable. She had prepared a lovely lunch that included tuna fish salad, crackers, fresh fruit, and unsweetened tea. There were fancy little cookies for dessert. My parents left around 4 p.m., hugging me tightly before leaving me—so tight that I could still feel the hugs an hour later. Before they arrived back in Louisville, I was missing them terribly, and yet I was excited to begin a life in a big city that I had only seen on television.

Ms. Jackson had given me all information concerning riding the bus to school. I had never ridden a city bus in my life, so she gave me step-by-step instructions. She reminded me that if I missed the 7:15 a.m. bus, I would be late for class. I did not have to worry about transferring to another bus as it was a straight shot from where I lived to the school. I was good to go!

Attending Dental Technology School in Atlanta, GA

The school had sent me three white uniforms that were to be worn to school. My mama had bought me white shoes that reminded me of nurses' shoes. Ms. Jackson also left the house to go to a modeling assignment with Nancy being picked up by another mom taking her daughter to the same school. I grabbed an apple, banana, and orange juice to eat after I got to school. Boy, I was already missing the hot breakfasts that my mama and Grandma Lula cooked every morning that included oatmeal or grits, bacon, eggs, biscuits, hot chocolate, or any number of other delicious hot meals.

The bus stopped, and I walked on, paying the fare of $.35. I sat as close to the front of the bus so that I would not miss my stop. I wondered how the bus driver would know where I needed to get off. I forgot to ask Ms. Jackson about that. At that point, I remembered what Grandma Maybelle had said:

> *"When in a place and you don't know what to do, find someone who looks like they know what to do and follow them—but be careful."*

I also felt I needed to send up a quick prayer to let Jesus know I needed help which I did quietly. The lady in front of me reached up and pulled on a chord that was to her right. The bus stopped at the next stop, and she departed the bus. Praise the Lord as I knew what to do. As I saw the school coming up, I pulled the chord, the bus stopped, and I was at my destination.

When I walked into the building, I saw other students dressed like me. I sat down at a table with a girl that was sitting alone. I spoke to her, and she spoke back to me. I told her my name, and she said her name was Wilma. After chatting for just a few minutes, I learned she was from the town of Dublin, GA. She had married her high school sweetheart before he left for Vietnam. As she explained that her husband was killed while serving over there, her eyes became full of tears. I told her I was sorry—she said she was too. We sat together in the class.

During the break, I met her cousin, whose first name was Bea. For some reason, I got an awful feeling about Bea even though she smiled a lot and was friendly. Since I liked Wilma, I knew that I would also have to deal with Bea for us to continue to be friends, so I did. The first day of school went by quickly, and it was time to go home. All of the students had to stand in the exact location to get on the right bus to go home. When I arrived home, no one else was there yet. I used my key and entered the apartment. There was no Mama, Daddy, or Grandma Lula to meet me to share my day and no warm meal already prepared. For just a moment, I was afraid as I had never been alone in my life. It took a few minutes to adjust, but I did, and I immediately changed clothes and began to look for something to eat. There was plenty of food in the refrigerator, so I made tuna fish salad while having grapes and apples. I also made sweet tea as Ms. Jackson had unsweetened tea. I finished my homework and watched a little television. Nancy arrived home around 7 p.m. as she had stayed with her friend's mom to do her homework and eat dinner. We talked for a while; however, Nancy had to be in bed no later than 8:30 p.m. whether her mom was at home or not. Ms. Jackson arrived home by 9 p.m. She asked me about the school, and I shared my day, and she shared how she had to do a swimsuit layout and had a dinner date with a friend. I was in bed by 10:30 p.m., thinking about my family as I drifted off to sleep.

I was beginning to get into the school routine even though I still missed my family very much. My mama and daddy called me on Friday afternoon at a little after 5 p.m., and I was so glad to talk to them. We were on the telephone for about an hour, and I shared every detail of what was happening with me. They listened attentively while also asking such questions as, "Are you eating solid food? Are you being safe?" And, of course, telling me, "Do not go anywhere without letting Ms. Jackson know because the city is different from Louisville. Remember to study every day so that you will make good grades. Ask Ms. Jackson if there is a church nearby as you need to go to church. Pray every day." The minute I heard from them, I was at total peace and knew that my world was okay. Grandma Lula even talked for a few minutes with me, which was a surprise to my parents, letting me know, "I am praying for you every day knowing that the Lord is watching over you." I could feel their love and support for me over the phone. They wanted to know if I needed anything, and I said that I did not. They had sent me some money in the mail, which I would receive by Monday. My parents also talked with Ms. Jackson, who assured them that I was no trouble to her at all and that she was glad to have me in her home. She also felt that I was a good influence on Nancy. My world was perfect again.

Are You a Maid?

One morning when boarding the bus, I noticed a woman watching me quite closely. She was a short Black woman with bold, black eyes that seemed to look right through me. I thought that she was a nurse as she wore a white uniform and white shoes. She looked stunning, with her uniform gleaming. She was sitting across from me on one aisle with my being on the aisle seat across from her. Finally, she spoke to me, and I spoke back. She asked me which family I was working for in the area. I told her that I was not working for any family but that I was attending school. She seemed astonished at my reply and shared, "Oh, I thought you were a maid working for the McNair family. But then you young folks don't like doing an honest day's work." For the first time in my life, I did not know what to say, so I did as my grandma Maybelle had said:

"If you can't say something good, say nothing."

Failing to Follow "My First Mind"

I met another girl at school, Lavonia, whom I liked very much and who had been born and raised in Atlanta. She was quiet and reserved and yet seemed to always know what to do in every situation. We worked together on a team project in class, causing us to spend a lot of time together during breaks. As we worked together, she told me that she liked the fact that I was "real." I asked her what that meant, and she said, "You have no problem being yourself without trying to pretend to be someone else." I thanked her and told her I did not see the point of pretending. My grandma Lula had said:

"Be yourself, and you never have to fake being someone else."

Bea was talking about a party that would take place at a girl's house on Saturday night. The girl lived in the Bankhead area of Atlanta. She was going and wanted Wilma and me to go with her. Immediately I did not have a good feeling about this party, and I did not have a clue about the Bankhead Highway area. Before I could voice my opinion not to go, Wilma said she would go if I would go. I did not want to lose Wilma's friendship, so I said I would go. Bea said she would pick me up in Buckhead at 8 p.m. I said "fine."

Lavonia was employed as a telephone operator working different shifts. She had heard about the party but had to leave school early on

Friday to go to work. I told Ms. Jackson that I was going to a party with some friends from school. She said that she was glad that I was doing something other than school. I told her I was meeting friends in Buckhead and that they would bring me back to that location. She liked the idea because Buckhead was a safe area with police on duty all the time. Cabs were also available until 3 a.m. I told her I would be home by 11 p.m. She said that was fine, but if I decided to stay out a little later, she expected me to be home by no later than midnight. I thanked her.

Daddy had always told me that I should make sure that I had enough money to return home by cab, even if someone had said they would take me somewhere and bring me back. The cab fare from Buckhead to where I lived in Sandy Springs was $12. I took $40 just in case I needed it. I arrived at Buckhead at 7:55 p.m., with Bea picking me up at 8 p.m. as promised. As we were making the drive to Bankhead, I noticed Bea smoking cigarettes and talking loudly, using profanity as I had never heard before. Even Wilma seemed somewhat surprised at Bea's behavior. Another thing I noticed was that we had been riding for more than forty minutes, but we were not at the party.

We finally arrived at the party at 9:15 p.m. with people drinking alcohol, smoking cigarettes that smelled funny, and some people looking like they were walking in a daze. I could hear my grandma's words ringing in my ears: "Never go against your first mind—it is almost always the right choice." By 10 p.m., I was looking for a way to get back home. I asked Bea what time was she planning on leaving the party. She replied, "I don't know, I just got here," and she walked away from me.

I asked one girl who appeared to be sober about how I could get a cab home. She started laughing and replied, "Girl, where are you from? Ain't no cabs out here, and if you call one, they ain't coming." I tried to find Wilma, but I could not. I also noticed women and men going to cars together and to different rooms in the house. One of the boys from school was also at the party; his name was John. He came over and started talking to me. I thought this was strange as he did not even speak to me at school. I was so scared and told the Lord that I would never be in this position again if He would get me out of this situation!

A miracle happened as I looked towards the door; Lavonia was walking in. I was so glad to see her. She came straight to me and asked, "Why did you come to this place? You don't even fit in with this crowd." I told her she was right. She told me to follow her to her car. When we got in the car, she told me not to ever come to this side of town again. "People get killed over here all the time. I must be back to work in an hour and a half, so I can't take you all the way home, but I can take you to Buckhead. Do you have enough money for a cab home?" I told her I had enough money for a cab, and I thanked her so many times for coming to my rescue that she told me not to say it again. She also said, "While Wilma is a nice girl, Bea is not, and I guess you already know now that she is not your friend and can't be trusted." I agreed. After Lavonia dropped me off in Buckhead and the cab ride home, it was 11:30 p.m. I forgot to ask her how she knew where I was, but it did not matter. I looked at this as a miracle—God had saved me, and I never ignored my "first mind" again. On Monday morning, Bea was her usual self, apologizing for what had happened. I had no more dealings with her at school, with Wilma also telling me that she would never go to another party with Bea. Lesson learned!

The Unexplained Police Stop

It was now March of 1971, and school was going well for me with my learning the city of Atlanta. Jim and I talked by phone at least twice a week and had been communicating like this since he took the job with the fabric company in October. He knew where I lived but felt that since I lived on the "white side of town," it was best for him not to come to the apartment. I was so busy with school that it was probably a sensible idea.

I was also making trips back home with friends as well as by the Greyhound bus. One of my former classmates, Henry, had a car and was also attending classes in Atlanta. He told me that Lorna and Marcia were also attending classes. We rode home together with everyone buying some gas even though Henry said there was no need to do so. The rideshare was going just fine until a police officer stopped us as we traveled through a small town about an hour outside of Atlanta. He never really said why he stopped us, but when he looked in the back and saw me in the car, he commented that Henry needed to watch who was riding in his car. While we did not pay any attention to this, I shared it with my daddy. He told me it was best for me not to ride with Henry anymore. When I asked him why, he shared, "If that police officer had decided that he wanted to say that you were doing something illegal, you would be in trouble with Henry, Lorna, nor Marcia having the ability to help you without being placed in trouble too. From now on, you will ride the bus home." I remember thinking that it had taken four years for there to be acceptance of Black students at the white high school. Four and one-half years had passed with positive change being made by the students but with others still feeling the same. Grandma Maybelle was right:

"Some people ain't goin' to change no matter how old they git."

Ms. Jackson Gets a Marriage Proposal and a New York Job Offer

On the third Sunday of April, Ms. Jackson asked that I sit with her in the kitchen as she had something to discuss with me. I knew that this was something different as Nancy was spending the weekend with a friend. She informed me that two important things had happened over the past week, and she wanted me to know about them in advance. The first thing was that her boyfriend had asked her to marry him, and she had been offered a modeling assignment in New York. The assignment would last for at least six months, with her having to leave for New York on June 10. She had stated that she would make living arrangements for me through September and that she would also talk to my parents to ensure they had peace of mind about the situation. While this was not in the contract with the school, she had stated that this was something she wanted to do because I was a joy to live with. She just wanted me to know in advance. Since the last day of school would be September 10, there was plenty of time.

I was really excited for Ms. Jackson because she was not only a nice person, but she was also a great mom, and she treated me like a member of her family. When I talked with my parents, they informed me that Mrs. Mason, my cousin's grandmother, had called to come to visit my cousins Martina, Victoria, and Wilson, who were living with my parents and Grandma Lula at the time. My cousins were the children of my mother's only sister Annette, separated from her husband, Wilson, Sr. No one knew where Wilson, Sr. was with my aunt Annette having to spend some time in a mental facility to receive help in dealing with her issues. When my parents shared that I was attending school in Atlanta, Mrs. Mason told them that I could live with her if I needed somewhere to live. She felt that since my parents had done so much for her son's children, this was the least that she could do for me. I asked my parents if I could think about this, and they had no problem with me doing so. I wanted to discover where Mrs. Mason lived and how far it was from the school.

Over the next two weeks, I had the opportunity to learn that Mrs. Mason lived in SW, Atlanta, which was also the black side of town. Jim's sister lived only five miles from Mrs. Mason's house, which meant we could see each other versus just talking over the telephone. I shared with Ms. Jackson that Mrs. Mason had invited me to stay with her and that I wanted to do so. My parents came to Atlanta on June 2 and helped me move to Mrs. Mason's home. By this time, Ms. Jackson had decided not to get married but to move to New York.

It was a bittersweet moment in my life as living with Ms. Jackson allowed me to build a relationship with Nancy, Ms. Jackson's only child. It was like having a little sister who admired me and listened to everything I had to say. I also shared with Nancy my family life as well as stories my grandmas had shared with me. She enjoyed these stories as she had only seen one of her grandmothers a few times. Ms. Jackson, Nancy, and I shed some tears and many hugs before I was off to my new living quarters. I knew I would miss them very much.

GRADUATION FROM DENTAL TECHNOLOGY SCHOOL AND MOVING FORWARD WITH MY LIFE

Living with Mrs. Mason was similar to living at home with my parents as there was a hot breakfast every morning before I went to school and dinner by 5 p.m. every day, including Sunday. Mrs. Mason and her husband Lincoln had been married for ten years, with Mrs. Mason working a part-time position at a dry cleaner to have something to do. Mr. Mason spent most of his days at a nursing home visiting old friends. Mrs. Mason gave me instructions about the bus service and having to change buses at the downtown bus transit location. I had my own room and plenty of space to study. I liked the house.

The neighborhood was different from Ms. Jackson's neighborhood, especially on the weekends. Boys were riding through the neighborhood playing loud music and people yelling at their children, husband, wife, or whomever all the time. It took a few days to adjust to this, but I did. I also asked Mrs. Mason if it was okay for Jim to come to see me. She looked somewhat stunned that I asked for permission. She said, "Of course, your boyfriend can come to see you—you live here. Why are you asking for permission?" I let her know that one of the things that my parents and grandmas had taught me was to have respect for everyone. Grandma Maybelle said:

> *"Always respect your elders, and this means people old enough to be your mama or daddy and old folks. The Bible tells you to do this, so do it!"*

Since I was living in her house, I felt I needed to know if it was all right for me to have visitors. She smiled approvingly at me and said, "Your parents have brought you up right! I know they must be so proud."

Jim came to see me on Saturday, and I introduced him to Mr. and Mrs. Mason. We sat outside and talked, then left to go to dinner and a ride to familiarize myself with the neighborhood. I was home by 10 p.m., as this is what I would have done if I was at home in Louisville. It was nice having the ability to see Jim and spend time with him as it had been months since we had seen each other. I still felt the same about him, and he felt the same about me. But I also focused on school to ensure that I would graduate with good grades.

Finally, September arrived, and I graduated from Dental Technology School. There was one thing that I knew for sure, and that was that I had no plans to be a dental technician. I was not too fond of the processes involved in making dentures and partials, even though these were tools that aided people in having beautiful smiles and eating food efficiently. Not too soon after graduation, Jim and I went to the courthouse and exchanged our wedding vows. We celebrated our marriage with a meal at the Atlanta downtown Walgreens before going to our very first apartment. There was no fanfare or expensive wedding, but we were happy. I had no idea how the sayings of my grandmas would affect my life as I moved from schoolgirl to wife and mother.

CHAPTER 3
GRANDMAS' PEARLS OF WISDOM BECOMING REALITY IN MY LIFE

Memories of my childhood and growing up are beginning to feel like so many years ago, even though I am still going back home and visiting my family. My grandmas constantly tell me how proud they are of me, and I feel like I am still that little granddaughter they helped raise. My family and Jim's family already knew each other, but with Jim and I getting married, there was a celebration of two families coming together. It was one of the best weekends ever. The people in the neighborhood decided to give us a reception which took place the third weekend after our marriage. It was more than I could have ever asked for with barbequed pork and beef, homemade dishes ranging from pork and beans, macaroni and cheese, turnip and collard greens, and the list goes on and on. There were more gifts than we could have imagined, with our marriage starting in perfect fashion. But the words of my grandma Lula loomed in the back of my mind:

> *"Marriage brings with it many troubles—spend time in prayer and make sure you hear from God before doing it."*

Consequently, I sent up an early prayer for God to watch over us and protect our marriage.

HAVING CHILDREN

It took only a little while for me to become pregnant, even though I did not know that I was pregnant. I felt tired and had morning sickness but paid no attention at all. Finally, I noticed that I was gaining weight and craving everything in sight, so my cousin took me to a doctor, and of course, the news of my pregnancy was announced. My mom and dad had mixed emotions about it as they believed that I was too young to have a baby, and my grandmas felt the same. But none of that mattered as I was pregnant, and Jim and I were extremely excited about it.

I worked as a file clerk with no heavy lifting, or anything involved. It was lunchtime, and Thea, the administrative assistant for Kent, my manager at the insurance company, had planned to eat at Krystal. As we were getting ready to leave, I quickly stopped by the restroom to discover some bleeding. Thea seemed concerned and told me to call the doctor. I made the call and was told to come to the doctor's office. When I arrived, they saw me immediately and explained that my body was attempting to begin labor. The plan was to admit me into the hospital and perform a surgery permitting me to reach a full-term pregnancy. I called Jim at work to deliver this most unexpected news. He told me that he was on the way to be with me. After that, I felt at least 100 percent better.

My Out-of-Body Experience

At a little past 2 p.m., I was admitted to the hospital. This was a new experience for me, and I was scared beyond reason. The doctor came in to explain what was happening to my body, with my only understanding being that I was going into labor, and they planned to try to prevent it by performing a surgery that involved placing a loop within me to stop the delivery. In that way, the baby would continue to grow with my body being able to handle it. But I began having contractions that continued to increase. Finally, the doctor informed me that I would give birth, and they began to prepare me for the event. By now, Jim had arrived and was allowed to see me for only a few minutes. I could tell by his expression that he was just as scared as I was, but he let me know that he loved me and that we would get through this just fine. I felt a lot better because of Jim's comforting words. I remember being placed on a bed and being taken to the operating room. I was given a mild sedative but could still hear all the different voices, including the doctor and the nurses as they quickly rolled me down the hall. When we arrived in the room, I felt my body and the pain that was occurring; however, suddenly, I felt my body separating with a part of me lifting toward the ceiling. As I was being lifted, I could see myself on the table and the doctors and nurses working on my body as they talked to each other. I was thinking, *I must be dead*, yet I was aware of everything going on. I heard a voice say to me, "No, you are not dead. Move your right hand." I followed instructions and saw my right hand moving. I remember that I no longer felt any pain and was not afraid anymore, feeling totally at peace. I did not understand how I was feeling these things, and yet I was feeling them. I do not know how long I was out of my body, but I know that I was. Just as quickly as I experienced being out of my body, I was back in my body, feeling the pain of childbirth. I have never forgotten this experience.

A Baby Girl is Born

Our little girl was born later that night two and a half months early, weighing in at two pounds thirteen and three-quarter ounces. The doctors had hoped that they could prevent me from giving birth so early, but they could not. I did not get a chance to hold my little girl nor give her a name. She was born being placed into an incubator and to emergency in an effort to keep her alive. Jim visited me, but I could tell that he was distraught. The doctors told me that they would do everything that they could to save her. I knew that my little girl was in a lot of trouble and that the only one that could save her was God. I remember lying in my room alone while feeling fear in a way that I had never known before.

Suddenly, I remembered what Grandma Lula said to me when talking to her on the phone after I left home: *"I am praying for you every day, knowing that the Lord is watching over you."* Since I knew God heard Grandma's daily prayer, I felt it was time for me to send up one for my baby girl. My words to God were simple because I had never been in a situation like this one. I said, "Lord, I don't know You like my grandmas or my parents, but I do know that You answer prayer. This prayer is for my little baby, who needs the help that only You can give. I promise You that if You let my baby live, I will take care of her and be the best mother that I can be." That was it. I fell asleep and was awakened by the pediatrician the following morning. He entered my room and said, "I don't know what you believe in or what prayer you prayed, but your baby is alive and improving, and we had nothing to do with it." Grandma was right—prayer works!

What a Difference a Baby Makes!

My parents were so excited to be grandparents, and of course, my grandmas were now great-grandmas. My little girl was named Sonya, and she was a ray of sunshine. Grandma Maybelle already had one great-grandchild, but Sonya was Grandma Lula's first, and Grandma Lula was speechless. Because Sonya was born prematurely, she stayed in the hospital to become healthier and gain weight. Miracles that only God could do continually happened as my little girl could not be spanked when born because her lungs were not fully developed. The doctors had to create a unique mouthpiece for her to aid in her breathing. During the night, she managed to cough up some mucus which became lodged in the cup. But the mucus lodged on the side of the cup without interrupting her breathing. She was so small, but she managed to be fed with a small bottle that the doctors found and that had a special nipple. Each day the nurses called me with good news concerning my baby's condition, with Jim and me seeing her every other day. The doctor told me that she would be in the hospital for at least ninety days, but God had a much better plan with Sonya coming home in fifty-two days, weighing five pounds and five ounces. Jim and I were so excited to bring our baby girl home with my cousin taking us to the hospital to pick her up. Everything had been set up for her arrival, including the baby bed, mattress, and more clothes than could be imagined. Since I had no brothers or sisters, I had no idea what to do, but I had faith that God would show me. The nursing staff had a little party as Sonya had also become *their* baby as they watched her grow so that she could go home with Jim and me. Some tears were shed, with all of them giving me much-needed advice and telling me to call if I needed any help once Sonya was home. I counted this as a special blessing from God as these people really cared about Sonya and us. I remembered Grandma Maybelle said:

> *"Nobody has to do nothin' for you or give you anything. If someone brings you a glass of water, be thankful cause they didn't have to do it."*

The years seemed to stand still as life was good for us. Jim worked as a mechanic for a moving company and worked on cars on the weekend with a brother-in-law. I worked with an insurance company and finally took a part-time job in retail. We were living quite well. Then, Grandma Lula came to stay with us for two weeks to be near her only great-grandchild and ensure the baby would be cared for properly. Those two weeks turned into nine years with Grandma Lula living with us until Jesus called her home. It was awesome having her with us!

As Sonya began to grow, I started thinking about another child. Jim and I talked about it and decided we would try for another baby. I remembered both Grandmas talking about the importance of prayer, and by now, prayer was a significant part of my life. But I knew I wanted a little boy the second time, so I started talking to God about that. One weekend when talking to my parents, I asked them if they were ready for another grandchild. They shouted, "*Yes!*" and we all laughed. I later talked to my dad in one of those "father-daughter" conversations, asking him if he regretted not having a son. His response was direct and to the point, as he said, "Your mom and I wanted three children, but it just didn't happen. We were glad to have you, and I never regretted that we did not have any more children. It would have been nice, but we were very glad to have you. Always know that God's plan is the best plan."

Nine years later, Karic Lewis was born with his first name being given to him by my cousin, his middle name was my dad's middle name, and of course, the last name was already in place. I will never forget calling my parents and telling them they had a grandson, and when I told them his name, the phone was completely silent. And while Karic was also born prematurely, he weighed four pounds and four ounces. I was allowed to go home, but he had to stay in the hospital to gain a little more weight. My parents came up to see him and stood side by side for a little over three hours, looking at him in the hospital nursery. Mama said Dad repeated his name at least a hundred times—my parents had a grandson!

My sister-in-law lived about twenty minutes from me and came by to spend some time with me so that I would not be alone once I returned home from the hospital after Karic's birth. This was most unusual for her as she really did not like to visit anyone with me being included in that group. I was on the phone sharing the news of the birth of our son with family and felt the need to sneeze. Blood went everywhere when I sneezed, and I was in shock. My sister-in-law jumped up and wrapped me in the covers that quickly became blood-soaked. She put me in the car and headed for the hospital. It took about ten minutes to get there, with us going to the emergency entrance. By the time I was in a hospital room, the doctor said I had lost a lot of blood and needed a blood transfusion immediately. I knew I needed Jesus quickly, and without hesitation, I immediately began to pray for myself as well as my son who was only a few floors away. Grandma Lula said:

> *"There will be times in life when things are happening that you do not understand. Don't ponder the situation; just pray and trust God."*

I would like to say that I was not scared or fearful, but that would be untrue. And there was no need to try to figure things out but to do as my grandma said—*trust God*. My prayer was simple, "Lord, I need you, and I am scared; please help me—Amen." The next thing I remember is the doctor saying that they would give me something to help calm me, and the nurse was inserting something into my arm. Within a few minutes, I felt different, and then I felt strange. I felt as though my body was being divided in half, with the right side being good and the left side being bad. I began to hear voices with my right-sided voice telling me to be calm and my left-sided voice telling me that I could fly. I did not realize I was having conversations aloud. After twenty-four hours of these conversations, I awakened to find myself strapped in bed, including my hands. A nurse in the room watched me very closely. When I asked her what happened, she told me that the Demerol caused me to hallucinate. Once everyone found out that I was fine, another nurse on the floor shared that people paid money to have that experience by buying drugs. I told her I never wanted to have that experience again. Demerol was later shown in my chart as a drug that I was never to be given again! Thank God for my grandma's prayers!

The Blessing of My Children

I loved being a mom as raising my children caused me to have a new appreciation for living. Hearing them laugh, cry, ask a million questions, play, fall, and the list goes on and on was a unique experience daily. Grandma Lula said:

> *"Children are one of the greatest blessings from God. And should you be blessed to see grandchildren, you have been doubly blessed. But God has blessed me to see a great-grandchild. I am too filled with joy to express what I feel!"*

But what I also found amazing was that my children were so different. Sonya was my *angel child* as she did not like getting spankings or being fussed at, so she did as she was told the first time; hence, the reason I wanted child number two.

Karic was made of an entirely different cloth. He was daring and loved to try to do anything. He was fearless and was a born explorer, always looking for something to get into. We always had some kind of animal around us, including a dog, cats, or birds. The animals were in total peace as long as Karic was inside the house; however, when he came outside, the animals scattered very quickly. By the age of two, he had been to the emergency room twice—once for running into the edge of the wall causing a lump to form in seconds on his forehead, and a second time for a piece of hard candy becoming stuck in his throat. If I had given birth to Karic first, Sonya would not have been born. And yet it was these two children that made my life complete. They are the greatest blessing that God has ever given me (other than Jesus Christ), and I am still reaping the blessings of these beautiful children right now!

Life in All Its Glory

My First Job

One thing about life that is learned very quickly is that it is an ever-evolving process. For example, my first job was working as a file clerk at an insurance company. On the very first day on the job, I knew I wanted to do something different career-wise; however, Grandma Lula said:

> *"Do not always desire to start at the top because there is something to be learned at the bottom. Working from the bottom up is better than starting at the top and falling down."*

I had no idea what this meant when she first told me; however, I took this to mean that I should work faithfully, show up to work on time, and do a good job; and so I did. Within six months, there was a position available for a Health Claims Assistant. I talked with Lynn, the lead claims manager, who was very nice to the customers and me. I asked her about the available position. She asked if I were interested and that if I was, she would love to train me. This sounded good to me, so we did training during my lunchtime not to interfere with my regular working hours. Within two weeks, she was pleased with my progress and talked to her manager, Kent, about my being moved into the position. He was somewhat hesitant but decided to give me a chance. The job was accessible to me, and I loved talking with the customers and helping them with their problems. Lynn began to provide me with some other responsibilities. She informed the company management that by taking on some added responsibilities, the Health Claims Assistant could quickly be promoted to the Claims Manager position. But I noticed that I did not see a raise in my paycheck from the new position. I checked with Lynn and found that she had completed the necessary paperwork and given it to Kent. In checking with Kent, he stated that it would take at least two weeks before seeing the pay increase. But I had already been working in the new position for six weeks. Kent told me not to worry as I would be back paid once the paperwork was completed.

Learning That People Will Lie to You without a Care

While I had always been taught to respect authority, I experienced a feeling on the inside that I had never felt before. In my heart, I believed that Kent was not truthful, and the feeling was not a good one. But I remembered what Grandma Maybelle said:

> *"Go with your first mind, and you won't go wrong—go with what you are feeling deep inside the first time as this is the right feeling leading to the right choice. To go against it brings trouble."*

When I got home, I talked to Jim about the situation. He felt that I should just wait until the next payday because there was nothing that I could do at this point but wait. The next payday came, and I still was not paid. Once again, Grandma was right! I knew that Kent had lied to me, and I knew that I did not want to talk to him again to hear more lies. I decided to look for another job. Within two weeks, I began working for a telecommunications company, making double the salary I had made for the insurance company. Lynn was happy for me even though she hated to see me leave. She confirmed my suspicion that Kent had lied and had never turned in the paperwork. Once I gave Kent my resignation, he "pretended" to be so sorry and that he would make sure that I was paid for the new position. I never received that money, but I moved forward without holding any negative feelings about it. It was a lesson learned that taught me how to listen to my heart, as my grandmas said.

God's Plan Being the Best Plan

I loved working at the telecommunications company as there were many opportunities. I held the position of an administrative assistant working for a regional manager. Mr. Johnson was genuinely friendly and helped me to learn the tasks relative to reporting that he needed. Ms. Timpson, the Executive Assistance, was very professional and knew the schedule of every manager in the office. She was the executive assistant to the VP and, as far as I was concerned, knew everything and could probably walk on water! She helped me learn about creating business letters, excel reports, memorandums, and everything associated with the administrative assistant position. She also liked the fact that I learned quickly. Within six months, I handled all reports for Mr. Johnson while also helping the two other assistants in the office with their duties. But I also noticed that Mr. Johnson was out of the office more playing golf with my preparing the reports and doing the meetings with the senior staff. While I had now been in the position for one year, I knew it was time to look at moving to another position as many of my manager's duties had become MY duties, and no one had mentioned a raise. Grandma Lula said:

"Know your worth and act accordingly because if you do not know your worth, someone else will tell you what you are worth, and they will usually place your worth less than what it actually is."

I met a girl named Billie, a secretary in the marketing department when I started with the company; however, she transferred to the installation department two months after starting. Since she had moved to another department, she could share with me how she made the transfer. Grandma Maybelle had said:

"When you need advice, talk to somebody you know has some sense. No good comes from grasping in the dark."

Her first advice was to keep my desire to transfer to another department to myself. If I shared that I planned to move, Mr. Johnson had the power to prevent it, and she knew that he would do just that. Her second tip was to tell me about electronics training that took place Monday through Friday, from noon to 1 p.m. on the top floor. The training was free and took place at this time so that anyone interested in the training could do so during their lunch hour. This was how she moved from being a secretary to becoming a switchman. Finally, she received advice from someone who had transferred and felt good to share the news with me. By receiving the training in advance of placing the transfer, the company viewed the employee as dedicated and motivated.

I followed her advice and received the needed electronics training from the company during my lunch hour and became a "frameman," or shall we say a "framewoman," within three months. I loved it, and I also found that it was great working with men versus women. Men asked direct questions wanting direct answers, which was what I enjoyed. Many of the women that I had worked with asked questions but questioned the answers. I did not have to think about saying something that might not be understood by this group which made working with them a lot easier.

But as you can imagine, something had to change what I believed was my perfect world. There were two Black managers in the department, with one being over the framemen (Eric) and one over the switchmen

(James). But during this time, the company was beginning to look at promotions for minorities, and my supervisor talked to me about a position where I would be a manager over the central office with framemen and switchmen. I told my supervisor that I needed to think about it. The benefits were fantastic as my salary would double and I would also have the opportunity to train continually, which I really liked. I talked to Jim about it, and he said whatever I decided was okay with him. I called my dad and talked with him about it, and my dad asked if I was coming home that weekend. I said "yes," and he said we could talk after he had time to think about it.

By coming home, I also had the chance to talk with my grandmas about it. Grandma Lula said:

> "This is a big decision, so you need to pray about it."

Grandma Maybelle said:

> "The Bible says before you do something count up the cost. The money sounds good but what will you have to do? Will you be over white folks and Black folks? You need to know everything before you make a decision. And don't forget to pray."

Daddy's advice was just like Grandma Maybelle's, as he had turned down the offer of promotion on his job because of the trouble he knew he would have by being the only Black manager at the plant. He also shared that the problem would come from the Black people, with the white people challenging everything he asked them to do. But my dad also said, "You have to make your decision based on what you want to do—not on what I didn't do. Just pray about it."

I prayed about it, and on Monday, my supervisor asked me if I wanted the position with my telling him I wanted to know about all the responsibilities that came with the position. There were many responsibilities that I knew I could handle; however, I learned that I would also be the manager of Eric and James. This was something that I did not feel would work out for me, so I decided to stay in my present position.

God Steps in without My Knowledge

I was thrilled with my life at this point. Jim had moved from the fabric plant to becoming a mechanic for a moving company. The pay was excellent, and he and our brother-in-law worked on cars on the weekend at our brother-in-law's house. Jim earned enough money to pay every bill, so any money I made was simply gravy. We saved and had money to spend. Buying gifts for my parents and grandmas was something I really enjoyed because all of them had been so good at giving to me all my life.

But even though I was incredibly happy at work, changes were beginning to take place at work that were a little annoying. We had to work longer hours with little notification and were about to switch to a new reporting system that was going to be somewhat challenging. I did enjoy challenges, but a few of the people that I worked with saw these challenges as a way to create problems that would affect future promotions. I remember Grandma Maybelle saying:

> *"Learn how to keep your mouth shut—there are times when people are not interested in hearing an opinion."*

I felt like this was one of those times. The job was enjoyable as long as we all worked together—not working together made the job negatively challenging.

Going with My Cousin to Apply for Her "Dream Job"

Since we would perform a special install over the weekend, we were given two days off through the week to make up for some of that time. I had no plans but to stay at home; however, my cousin Dana who moved to Atlanta when I did, had always wanted to be a flight attendant. She had heard that one of the major airlines in Atlanta was hiring and wanted me to go with her for the job. This sounded good to me, so I agreed. Dana and I were very close, with her visiting me daily as she lived down the street from our apartment. She was also Sonya's Godmother, so it is easy to see her importance to me.

She picked me up at 7 a.m. to go and apply for the job. Both of us were dressed casually versus wearing a suit and being all dressed up for the interview. This also gave me time to ask her what a flight attendant did and why she wanted to do that job. She told me that the title of "flight attendant" was new, with the old term being "stewardess." These were the people who worked on the airplanes. The pay was between $12 to $15 an hour. I told her that I could understand why she wanted this job as the pay was great! We got to the office for the interview by 7:30 a.m., with at least thirty people already in line. By the time we parked and took our place in line, there were at least fifty people in line. I had never seen so many people applying for a job. I asked Dana if she thought that by the time they got to her, the job would still be available. She said, "Oh yea, as they have at least 120 positions available."

We noticed a girl coming toward us with applications in her hand for applicants to fill out for the flight attendant position. She explained what was needed to be attached to the application. Dana received the application and began to fill it out. The girl gave me an application, and I told her that I was just coming with my cousin for moral support. The girl looked at me, smiled, and said, "Well, that sounds good, but what would it hurt for you to fill out an application? You might get the job!" Dana looked at me and agreed, so I filled out the application.

By 9 a.m., the interviewers called people by name to be interviewed. The room where all of us were sitting was so quiet that you could have heard a pin drop. People were nervous, and some people even looked to be scared. Dana and I were also quiet since everyone else seemed to be focused on hearing their name being called. My name was called, and I went in to be interviewed, leaving Dana in the waiting room.

The woman who interviewed me was amicable and professional. She asked several general interview questions and noticed that I had a small child as Sonya was only slightly over two years old (at this time, Karic had not been born). She looked at me and said, "I see that you have a small child. This job involves traveling every week. If your child were to become extremely ill, do you have someone who could take care of her?" In my head, I could hear my grandma Maybelle's voice as she had said:

> *"Make a habit of telling the truth even when the truth may not be pleasant. Lies always catch up with you and you do not please God with lies."*

Grandma Lula said:

> *"Jesus said, 'You will know the truth, and the truth will set you free.' Always walk in the truth, and you will set a path in life that will bring you happiness even when the truth is not pleasant."*

Even though I was in an interview with my grandmas being over one hundred miles away, I could hear their voices as though they were with me. I looked at the woman interviewing me and said, "Yes, I do have someone who could take care of my daughter; however, if my daughter were extremely sick, I would take care of her myself. While the job is of importance, my child is of greater importance to me."

This woman looked at me and smiled. She said that she liked that I was honest and that I looked directly at her when answering the question. She asked two more questions and told me that I would be moving to phase two of the interview process. I was directed to another room with about ten people being in the room. I did not see Dana and could not leave the room to check to see where she was at this time.

One of the women in the room looked at the rest of us and asked, "Are you guys as stressed as I am right now?" The question broke the ice in the room, with people agreeing and admitting they were nervous. Another person said, "If I don't get this job, I don't know what I will do. I want it sooo bad." I looked at her and told her that while this may be her dream job, if not hired, she would simply look for another job. I also shared, "My grandmother told me that life can be full of disappointment, but you learn how to overcome it and move on." The girl sitting next to me agreed, saying that she had another interview with an accounting firm later that day and hoped that she would be able to keep that appointment in case this job did not work out.

Within twenty minutes, I was called in for the second interview, which consisted of a review of past work experience and questions concerning how to handle specific passenger issues. I passed this phase and was told that I was moving into the third and final phase of the interview process. This phase involved filling out paperwork for the airline while being informed that there would be a six-week training process with all trainees living at a hotel, even if you had an apartment or home in the Atlanta area. In this manner, everyone would be together without fearing being late because of traffic.

We were led back to the first waiting area with Dana waiting for me. I could tell by her facial expression that she did not get the job, and she could guess that I did get the job. I asked her what happened, and she stated that she was too tall as there was a height limit of 5'8" and she was 5'11". I would receive a call from the airline informing me when I would start. Dana was so happy for me with us sharing a celebratory lunch. I guess her grandma must have taught her what my grandma Lula had said to me:

> *"Always be happy for others even when what you may have wanted didn't happen."*

I hated she did not get this job as it was her dream. This was definitely God's plan for me because I never had ever thought about being a Flight Attendant.

Life-Changing at the Speed of Light

When I got home, I realized what had happened. Oh my God! I have a job with one of the biggest airlines in the world as a flight attendant. I will travel around the world as a job!

Suddenly, I was terrified and excited at the same time. When Jim came home from work, I shared this news with him. He was also excited and scared. We discussed what life would be like with me living in a hotel for six weeks. But there were not any problems relative to Sonya as my grandma Lula had been living with us, keeping Sonya since she was born. I was always thankful for this but even more grateful now. I was told that the airline would call me to let me know when training would begin while also allowing me to give a two-week notice to my present employer. As I shared the news with Grandma Lula, she said:

"I will be praying for you with this job, and I want you to remember to be proud of who you are and where you came from—never forget that."

I did not understand why Grandma said what she said, but I kept the saying in my heart. Through the years, I learned that my grandmas knew what they were talking about even when I did not understand.

The Phone Call and the Letter Arrive

The phone call came within two weeks, with my giving a two-week notice to the telecommunications company. The official letter arrived one week later. I knew I would miss these wonderful people I had worked with for nearly two years; however, I was excited about beginning a new career that I never imagined could happen.

Facing Personal Challenges

As the training process moved forward, I learned about the other people in the class. There were 205 flight attendant trainees, the largest class the airline had ever had in training at one time. Two hotels were used to house the trainees, with my being assigned to the larger hotel. I met people from Chicago, North Dakota, Los Angeles, New York, and Atlanta. It was so interesting talking with these girls about their lives and experiences. There were also a few men in the class, which I thought to be unusual as I was surprised to see men desiring to do the job. Chalk this up to my being from the country, I guess.

By the third week, we learned that about twenty trainees had been terminated because of smoking marijuana in their rooms. I could not believe that people would be this ignorant. With this happening, everyone else ensured that they obeyed every rule. The class work was not difficult as there were rules and regulations relative to the Federal Aviation Administration (FAA) and the airline that had to be strictly followed. By week five, we were to practice rescue in water with life vests and life rafts. I was terrified as I had taken swimming lessons when I was eight with someone pushing me into the deep side (six feet). I remember going to the bottom of the pool and being unable to breathe while being scared. Although the lifeguard rescued me, I never wanted to take swimming lessons again. Now I had to participate in this exercise or fail in completing the training.

My roommate, Shena, could tell that I was scared about something, so eventually, I had to tell her that I did not know how to swim. She assured me that since we would be wearing life vests, the process would be easy; however, I was not convinced. I remembered what my grandmas said:

"Never forget to pray—you need Jesus all the time."

When we went to bed, I prayed to God, *"Please, please, please, send someone to help me because I need help bad. I hate to admit it, Lord, but I am scared, and I would hate not to make it to the end with success—AMEN."*

The following day, we arrived at the swimming pool area with the instructors assigning partners for the exercise. My partners were Rick and Peter (not one person, but two). When we were getting in position for the exercise, I told Rick that I could not swim and that I was scared. He looked at me and smiled, telling me, *"...you remind me of a girl I met at a summer camp. She was also scared of water, but I was able to teach her how to swim, so don't worry about it. I've got you."* Rick's words made me feel so peaceful inside. And although I was still a little scared, there was more peace than fear. The exercises involved swimming from one end of the pool to the other while assisting a passenger and practicing entering the raft from the water. With God's grace, Rick, and Peter, I succeeded in completing the class. My grandmas were right—it was particularly important to pray and to remember the prayer being answered! I remained close to these two men for many years.

Graduating as a Flight Attendant

Graduation day was an exciting event with friends and family attending. My parents participated in every event that I was in my entire life. Whether it was the play "Cinderella," where I was the lead, singing in the church choir, singing Christmas carols, or having a one-liner in a church play, I knew that my parents were front row center with my grandmothers sitting in the second row. But my husband was also present, dressed, and looking fine! My graduation was no exception, except that both of my grandmothers were a little under the weather and did not make the trip to Atlanta, GA. Each of them was now getting older and had to take special care of themselves when feeling a little ill. My parents were all smiles as my wings were clipped on, and my husband blew me a kiss. I felt that I was standing on top of the world. We went out to dinner to continue the celebration with my parents spending the night. We had breakfast together the following day with my parents driving home. Since Grandma Lula was at my mom's house, Sonya returned with them. Jim and I had an exciting time celebrating my new position! I also remembered something that Grandma Maybelle said:

"If you have doubts before you start something, think twice about starting it. Finish what you start—that is important."

God had allowed me to start and finish flight attendant training, and for that, I was most grateful as well as thankful.

The Real Life of a Flight Attendant

The uniforms were very nice, making anyone wearing them look great. Having a uniform to wear meant not having to choose something to wear to work daily. It was also a bit of a challenge wearing high heels every day, but I liked the look. But I was unprepared for the erratic schedule that involved flying at 5 a.m. in the morning and flying all night the next day. In the 1970s, the job was considered glamourous; however, believe me, there is nothing glamorous about being called at 2 a.m. to sign in at 2:45 a.m. to fly to Kansas City, Cleveland, or Cincinnati. I shall also never forget about the trips to Detroit on an L-1011 at 3 a.m. being completely full of passengers, all requiring service within one and a half hours. These flights were always assigned to the reserve flight attendants who had no seniority.

Within a month, I was exhausted yet still loving the job. While I thought the training pay was exceptional, receiving my first paycheck as a flight attendant was unbelievable. Jim and I could now buy practically whatever we wanted while also paying off bills that we had accumulated. Within six months, we had moved into a much fancier (and more expensive) apartment complex that I used to look at when coming to Atlanta to attend school. I was exposed to designer clothes, shoes, jewelry, and cars. And while I had the money, I also experienced chronic sinus issues, colds, and other ailments. While at this time being a flight attendant was often viewed as exciting, there were also some negatives, such as being away from home, missing my baby and husband, and being tired when I was at home. It was at this point that I remembered Grandma Lula saying:

> *"Life has tradeoffs—a job may offer more money but takes away your time from your family. Another job offers less money but gives you more time with your family. Keep your life in balance, Connie—that is what is important."*

At this point, I was so tired I could not think, but I knew that my life would change for the better once I was holding a line versus being on reserve. Holding a line meant knowing when I would be going to work and when I would be coming home. Being on reserve involved being on call twenty-four hours a day for at least five days a week. And since the airline did not allow the use of beepers, the reserve had to be at home to answer the phone when *Scheduling* called to assign a trip.

A View of Arrogance versus Humility

I learned quickly how people could be so pretentious and feel the need to do so. The flight attendant job allowed the interaction with the rich and famous, entertainers, movie stars, producers, directors, government officials, sports players, and owners; the list is endless. The majority of these people were nice, but when you met a jerk, he or she was a colossal jerk. One incident that stands out concerns a well-known baseball team. The owners and the majority of the players had boarded the aircraft. As the flight attendant in charge, I was told by the captain that one of the players would be arriving shortly and that the flight would be delayed until his arrival. About forty minutes later, a chartered bus drove close to the aircraft, being surrounded by another bus filled with reporters. As the door of the first bus opened, a single player stepped off the bus surrounded by reporters. Questions were being asked, with the player taking his time to answer. The other players just looked at this process with disgust on their faces. About fifteen minutes later, the player finally boarded the flight. He acted as though he was the only player of importance. I thought about something my grandma Maybelle said:

> *"Be humble, not haughty—for the haughty people tend to fall very hard with no one caring about it."*

I could only imagine how the other players must have felt seeing this one player being interviewed as though he was the whole team.

During the flight, the player constantly demanded attention and ignored the other players. His actions caused a delay in service, which meant that I had to interact with him. I explained that we were responsible for serving the entire team, not just him. He informed me of who he was and that he was particularly important. I informed him that each passenger was important to me and that my job involved treating everyone equally. I also asked him if he had a relationship with his grandmother in his life—he looked at me and asked, "Why?" I said, "Because my grandma taught me that it was important to be humble versus arrogant. It doesn't seem as though you understand what that means." He looked at me as though he could choke me, but he was quiet the rest of the flight. Thank you, Grandma!

Important Memories

All of us have memories that seem to stay with us, and when looking at my flying career, I remember a few unique events that are more than special even today. Traveling within itself brings with it the opportunity to learn about people, other countries, diverse cultures, and learning from each other. But what I remember most concerns how my career with the airline brought about opportunities for my family.

Grandma Lula's First Flight

The main event was my grandma Lula flying for the first time. She had a sister in Detroit, MI, that she had not seen for several years and began talking about her more regularly. Aunt Thelma and Grandma Lula were awfully close as sisters, but as the years passed, they had not seen each other. I asked Grandma Lula if she would like to fly to see her sister and that if she did, I would accompany her. Grandma Lula always thought before speaking, so she told me that she would let me know. Two days later, Grandma Lula told me that she would fly.

I do not know who was more excited, Grandma or me. The flight was non-stop from Atlanta, GA, to Detroit, MI. Lunch would be served with my ordering Grandma a special meal to ensure she would eat onboard. Her seat number was 1F, with her sitting by the window. I told the flight attendants that this was my grandma and to lay on the charm and that they did. Since my grandma was a slow eater, they ensured that the minute the "Fasten Seat Belt" light was turned off, her meal would be served. She looked out of the window with awe on her face. I asked her how she liked flying, and she said, "I am not sure yet, but I will let you know." With that statement being said, she looked at me with a smile. I knew she liked flying, and when she saw the meal, she said, "This food looks good." The meal included baked chicken with yellow rice and gravy, a green salad with ranch dressing, a roll with butter, and baked apples. I told her to go for it, and she did. Grandma always ate really slowly, so I knew that she probably would not finish the meal. Finally, she looked at me and said, "I cannot believe I am flying on an airplane. The Lord is still doing miracles for this ole gal, and I am most thankful." I gave her a big hug, and she smiled. The captain made the announcement that we were on descent into Detroit. Grandma looked at me and said, "We are almost there already? I was just beginning to enjoy this flying thing!" The flight attendant came to take away the meal, and we prepared for landing. When we landed and Grandma saw Aunt Thelma at the gate, they each began to shed a few tears and hugged each other for a long time. The joy that I felt seeing this happen is beyond words. I stayed the weekend with Grandma Lula staying for two weeks. I had taken time off to be at home so that my grandma could have a good visit. Grandma Lula talked about this trip for the rest of her life!

Mom and Dad's First Flight

My mom and dad had taken many trips by car over the years but had never been on an airplane. I had flown two years before realizing that

I could fly for free and that my family could also fly for a minimal amount; the joy of being young and unaware! Yet this was a good thing because I had the opportunity to learn how to get around in different cities as well as benefit from the many discounts that were given to airline personnel. Jim and I had always made trips with my family, with the airline offering even better opportunities. When I asked my parents where they wanted to go, they were so excited that it took them a week to decide. They chose to take a trip to San Francisco, CA.

As we began planning the trip, I could tell that something was on my dad's mind. Since my mom had not mentioned anything to me, I knew that this was something that my dad was experiencing by himself. Finally, one Sunday afternoon, about a week before we were to leave, my dad said he wanted to talk to me about something. We always went for rides together to talk about everything, so this was nothing new to me. Finally, my dad shared that because of my job, he did not want to embarrass me when traveling. He said, "*You are around a lot of rich and important people. I am not educated like these people, and I do not want to say something to make you ashamed of me.*" I let my dad finish all that he had to say without interrupting him (something he had done for me when I was having the many challenges that young girls have when growing up). He ended by saying that it would be fine for Mama and me to go, and he could stay home. I looked at my dad and said, "*You are my dad and have done everything for my benefit. There is nothing that you could do to embarrass me. I love you, and we are going to have lots of fun. I am so proud to be your daughter!*" I remember the look of relief on his face still. We got an ice cream cone and brought some ice cream back for Mama, and Dad and Mom finished packing.

We arrived in San Francisco, CA, on a Friday at 10 a.m. and stayed there for a week. My parents were so excited with Jim and me, allowing them to decide what we did and where we ate. My dad looked at my mom and said, "Baby doll, we are walking on 'The Streets of San Francisco,'" which was the name of a television series that we all watched together. Walking the hilly streets of San Francisco was like a dream come true to them. We rode on the streetcars, ate at a restaurant called "Pam Pam's" for breakfast that served hot chocolate in a huge cup with a fancy chocolate cookie, and then visited Alcatraz. Sonya also had a great time, even though she was only four at the time. This was only one of the many trips that my parents enjoyed during my twenty years with the airline.

Jim's First Trip

Even though I was on reserve, there were times when I had enough notice about an upcoming trip to make plans. I had been assigned a trip to Santa Monica, CA, with a forty-eight-hour layover. The hotel where the airline crew would stay had access to the beach, which was perfect. Since the flight departed on a Friday, this meant the crew would have Friday night, all day Saturday, and Sunday morning at the hotel. Jim had the weekend off, which meant that he could go on the trip with me if the flight were not full. The flight had available seats, with Jim going on the flight with me. This was the best trip that Jim and I enjoyed together. We walked on the beach, went shopping, and spent some quality time together. This mini-vacation gave us some time to be together in a very romantic atmosphere, with both of us reconnecting with each other. We arrived back in Atlanta on Sunday evening around 8 p.m., with Jim having plenty of time to rest before returning to work on Monday.

A NEW WORLD OF OPPORTUNITIES

As a flight attendant, I was exposed to all types of opportunities, especially regarding different careers. From the time I was six years old, lying on my stomach and watching our black and white television, I dreamed of being an actress. I remember watching Elizabeth Taylor and the numerous roles she played so well. While there were other actresses on television, Ms. Taylor was just so outstanding to me. I remember asking my mom if there were any Black actresses because I did not see any on television. My mom said that there were some Black actresses but not that many. I told my mom that I wanted to be an actress. My mom just looked at me and smiled with Grandma Lula saying:

> *"Think of being something else just in case you don't become that actress."*

As I grew older, I saw Peggy Fisher in the series "Mannix" and Diahann Carroll in the series "Julia." This sealed the deal for me in desiring to become an actress at the tender age of fifteen. But as I grew older, I realized that I wanted a family more than I wanted to be an actress, thereby pushing this idea to the very back of my mind. Watching my mom and Grandma Lula prepare dinner before my dad came home and watching Grandma Maybelle cook for all of us let me see firsthand how important family was to life. But I also noticed that cooking for the holidays was the best time ever, and I loved being in the kitchen with my family as we prepared to celebrate Jesus and family.

But now that I was a flight attendant, I not only had access to Hollywood but to the world while meeting and having opportunities to talk to famous actors, actresses, kings, civil rights leaders, congressmen, senators, musicians, producers, and directors, gaining not only wisdom but also an understanding of so many different subjects. Since I was married and had given birth to my daughter and son, I felt I could try this acting bug. Grandma Maybelle said:

"Live your life and do the things you want to do as long as those things don't bring hurt to anybody. You don't want to grow old and look back with regrets because once you are old, you are old and can't go back."

Grandma Lula said:

"Life has been created to live. Place your values in God and family and let God guide you on life's choices. While you need money to live, never place a job or money before God and family. If you do, you will have regrets that will last a long time."

I had written my "Oscar" winning speech in 1972, so now was the time. When I talked to Jim about what I wanted to do, he said, "*Go for it. I would not have any problems living in LA with an actress.*" That was all I needed to hear. I took soap opera acting classes in New York and studied acting in Los Angeles. I was on my way to success. After two years of classes, I believed I was ready to launch!

The Conversation That Changed My Direction

My acting instructor, who went by the name of JC, had been working diligently with the class as there was a director who was a close friend who would allow us to audition for an upcoming movie if he were pleased with what he saw. I was utterly excited as I could see myself moving closer to that Oscar. The film would star several big-name actors with plans to allow a few unknown faces. JC had talked with a few of us that would be allowed to audition for this director while giving us guidance so that everyone realized just how important this opportunity would be to us. Out of a class of twenty students, six of us were chosen.

I had come to LA a day early to work with John, another student, as we worked well together and created absolutely phenomenal energy. We practiced distinct roles and scheduled a meeting with JC later that afternoon. JC also gave us different scripts from what we had practiced before, giving him an idea of our growth. It was a fantastic experience allowing us to see how much we had grown. JC was not easy to please as he was tough on all of us, letting us know that acting as a career was not just about acting but was also about business. Without keeping this in mind, one could fail even with solid acting ability. We were overjoyed when JC told us we were ready for the audition.

As we were getting ready to leave, JC told me that he wanted to talk with me. John told me that he would wait to go with me so that we could grab a bite to eat. JC sat down and began talking to me, saying:

"Connie, you have come a long way in this class, and I know that you are ready for this audition. But I want you to do me a favor, please."

I answered, "Okay, what?"

JC continued, "Go home and forget about a career in acting. When I first met you, I felt that you were 'acting' as you were always laughing and being pleasant to everybody. Your topic of conversation was always your family, and I thought, 'Let's see how long this act will last.' But you were not acting. You believe in things like being honest and helping people and treating people right. You have true feelings for people and have no problem helping anyone who needs it, and being truthful is your lifestyle. You have no problem admitting you are wrong and accepting responsibility for any mistakes you make. To be frank about it, I did not believe anyone acted like this anymore—but I was wrong. Hollywood will chew you up and spit you out without thinking about it. Go home and be the mother and wife that you love being. What you have now is far greater than what can be gained with an acting career."

I was so hurt by what he said. For the first time in my life, I had no words to speak. But in my heart, I knew he was right even though I did not want to accept it. I waited until John and I arrived at the little eatery down the street before sharing with John what JC said. John just looked at me and smiled, reminding me of how hard we had worked to get to this point. John was from California and told me that an opportunity like this one would probably never happen again. When I arrived back at the hotel and went to my room, I broke down in tears crying myself to sleep. I remembered that Grandma Maybelle said:

> *"Child, life can deal you some hard blows—you just have to trust King Jesus to bring you through."*

That was the end of my pursuit of an acting career with the belief that King Jesus would bring me through.

CHAPTER 4
LOSING MY GRANDMAS

Even when looking at the challenges that came as I lived my life, I always had my parents and my grandmas to talk to for advice. While I never took this fact for granted, it had become as routine as drinking a glass of water; however, I noticed that as I talked to my grandmas, their conversation would always end with them discussing leaving and going to be with Jesus. This was not a conversation that I wanted to have, so I would always manage to turn it around. But no matter how I changed the subject, my grandmas would change it back. I would begin to feel sad inside, yet I knew they would leave one day.

GRANDMA LULA

Grandma Lula had a younger sister in Brunswick, GA, that she liked to visit. Aunt Valarie was a soft-spoken woman who looked like Grandma Lula. Whenever we saw her when I was a child, we greeted one another with a long hug and a kiss that made me feel so warm inside. Aunt Valarie's daughter, Regina, would always come to visit, bringing her son Dusty. I loved playing with Dusty because he always liked to do something exciting and different with my following his lead. I loved visiting Aunt Valarie; we did so at least twice a year for as long as I can remember. When Sonya was three years old, Grandma Lula decided she wanted to visit Aunt Valarie. My mom and dad were on vacation, so they took Grandma to Brunswick and brought Sonya back with them. I planned to fly to Brunswick the following weekend as I had some time off. This would give me some quality time with Aunt Valarie and Grandma Lula before flying to Augusta to pick up Sonya from Mom and Dad's house and bring her to Brunswick for a visit.

I was on a trip and arrived in Atlanta with my supervisor meeting me at the gate. Since this was not usual, I knew something was wrong. She informed me that my mother had called, stating that my grandma Lula had a stroke and had been rushed to the hospital. There were no other details at this time. I caught the first flight to Brunswick with my parents picking me up at the airport. Sonya was with them, so we went directly to the hospital. When we arrived, my mom met with the doctor. He stated that Grandma's condition was stable but that she had not made any movement since being admitted to the hospital, so they were unsure how severe the stroke had been. They had run some tests and were waiting on the results. I was completely numb inside and scared of losing my grandma. I remembered Grandma Lula saying:

"Be mindful of how you live your life so that when Jesus calls you home, you are ready."

I took time by myself to talk to God as I had a good bit of practice. My prayer was direct and to the point, as I prayed, "Lord God, You have answered so many prayers for me over the years, and now I have yet another one. My grandma Lula needs Your help. I know she is old and has lived a good life, but if You would permit it, please give her some more time for me—In Jesus Name, AMEN."

We were finally permitted to see Grandma with my mom and dad going in the room first so that I could sit outside with Sonya. They were probably only in the room for a few minutes, but it seemed like hours to me. The nurse came out to speak with me and told me that I could go in, and she would sit with Sonya. But when she reached for Sonya, there was a bit of resistance from Sonya. I shared with the nurse that my daughter was the great-granddaughter of my grandma. The nurse looked at me, smiled, and said, "Maybe this little girl is what she needs. Take her in to see your grandma but I cannot let you stay in the room too long as small children are not permitted in the rooms." I thanked her and walked into the room. Grandma looked just like she always did, with her beautiful gray hair shining and her face beautifully wrinkled, caring, and loving, but she was not moving. Sonya ran from the door to the bed, looked at Grandma Lula, and said, "Come on, Granny, I want you to get up and play with me." We looked at Grandma as her eyes became teary. She moved her head slightly in Sonya's direction and whispered, "Alright," and moved her hand very slowly, moving in the direction of Sonya's tiny hand. Sonya placed her hand in Grandma's hand with the nurse seeing this at the hospital room door. The nurse ran and got the doctor with the doctor asking us to leave the room so he could examine my grandma.

The doctor looked at my mom and said, "This is nothing short of a miracle. It appears that some of the paralysis is temporary as we are now seeing movement in your mother's arms, and she is moving her neck back and forth. The movement is only slight, but it is movement. It will probably take a little time, but she appears to be recovering." Within two months, Grandma Lula was back at home. She was moving a bit slower but was talking just like always. I visited her weekly while in the hospital with my mom and dad bringing her home when I was at work. We had a celebratory dinner the following Sunday with Grandma enjoying the day. This was my realization of what she had been trying to tell me about leaving. While I had always appreciated my grandma Lula, this incident helped me to begin preparing for the day that she would really be gone.

The Discussion with Grandma Lula after Returning Home

After being home for a month, Grandma appeared to be the same except for moving a bit slower when she walked. She had also spent a few weeks in rehabilitation learning how to walk and talk again. The doctor said this was a precautionary measure and that grandma had done well. I was coming home every weekend to spend time with Grandma and for her to see Sonya as watching the two of them together brought much enjoyment. I was now flying trips where I could be home every day to take care of Sonya, with Jim working daytime hours and my flying quick night turnarounds.

As I prepared to go back to Atlanta on Sunday afternoon, Grandma and I sat outside under the beautiful tree in my mom and dad's backyard, which was something we did all the time. Grandma looked at me and said, "Well, I know that since I have had the stroke, you are probably afraid for me to be with Sonya by myself."

I looked at her and said, "No, we are not afraid for you to be with Sonya alone, but we do not want anything bad to happen to you again while having you worry about Sonya."

I could tell she had more to say, so I asked, "What do you want to do, Grandma?"

She looked at me with a smile and said, "I want to come back to your house to be with you, Sonya, and Jim. That baby means so much to me at this time in my life."

We toasted our glasses of lemonade together, and I said, "Let's get packed for you to go with me."

Grandma smiled and yelled to Sonya, "Come on, gal, we are going home."

Since Jim and I were at home at all times, we knew that Grandma Lula would be fine living with us as she did in the past, with our also having the ability to watch over her and Sonya.

Grandma Lula's Last Ride Home with Sonya and Me

It had been several years since she had the stroke, with Grandma moving somewhat slower as time passed. Grandma always liked to go back home to Louisville on the first of each month as she was paid her monthly stipend that came in the mail, and she wanted to buy a few things (mainly for Sonya). It also allowed her to see Grandma Maybelle, Cousin Emma, and a few of the ladies at church she had known for many years. Sonya was now eight-and-a-half years old, going to school and growing up fast to Grandma. I noticed that Grandma was packing many of her clothes as we prepared to go home. When I asked why she was packing so much, she said, "Well, girl, I have not worn some of these clothes for a long time, so I think I will take them home." I said, "Okay," and kept putting things in the car.

As we prepared to get in the car, Grandma took a minute, looked around, and said, "I am so thankful for you and Jim and for the two of you letting me be a part of Sonya's life. Thank you!" I told her that she would always be part of our lives. We rode home, stopping to get something to eat along the way. Grandma loved stopping along the way as we laughed and talked about many different things. Since it was a Friday afternoon in Atlanta, GA, traffic was awful, but Grandma did not mind at all. She told me that this gave us some extra time together. I agreed.

We had the usual great weekend, and I noticed that Grandma was not packing to go back with me on Sunday. When I asked her why, she told me that she wanted to stay home this week and spend time with Mom and Dad. This was nothing unusual, so I told her I would pick her up the following weekend. She smiled at Sonya playing with her as usual. As we backed out of the driveway to leave for Atlanta, I took a look back to wave at everyone, but when I looked at Grandma, I had a strange feeling that I cannot describe. She was smiling and waving at us, and I just pushed that strange feeling aside.

I trusted God to bless us with a second child at this time and prayed specifically for a son. I had been on birth control pills for seven and one-half years, with the doctor telling me it would probably take some time for me to conceive again. About one month later, I woke up having nausea and feeling very tired even though I had a good night's rest. I ignored this feeling and started my day flying a daytime turnaround with Jim having the day off. At the end of the trip, I came home feeling the same way for the next few days and gave my doctor a call. I was given a pregnancy test to discover I was indeed pregnant. I shared the news with Jim, and we decided to stay home the coming weekend to celebrate the pregnancy and would go to Louisville the following weekend to tell our families. We went out to dinner, followed by an evening of dancing. It was a very romantic time.

The Phone Call That Changed Everything

I was taking a nap when the phone rang. My mom told me that Grandma Lula had another stroke that was more severe than the one she had several years ago. When Jim came home, we left for Augusta as Grandma had been taken to the hospital there for better treatment. Sonya went into the room with us, but Grandma did not make any movement at all this time. The doctor assured us that she was not in any pain and that they would do everything possible to ensure she was comfortable. I also noticed that my mom appeared to be worried, which was something that very seldom happened. Jim seemed to be scared, and I could see tears coming to his eyes. He told me that he had to go to the car. I knew he had to get away, so I just said, "Okay." Jim loved both of my grandmas, but he and Grandma Lula had an exceptional bond because of her living with us for eight years.

The news of a new baby coming had mixed emotions as everyone was glad a new life was coming but sad that it appeared that Grandma Lula's life was slowly coming to an end. Grandma Lula was transferred from the hospital to the nursing home facility for the disabled as she could not do anything for herself without help. The facility was near my mom and dad's home, so they went to see Grandma every day after work. Jim, Sonya, and I came home every weekend and spent time with Grandma Lula. I missed hearing her voice when I talked to her and the nods she would give me, letting me know in her unique way that she understood what I was saying. But most of all, I missed the talks we had when she was living with us, hearing her tell Sonya to move over when they laid down for naps and at night when they went to bed. I cried and cried and cried until I had no more tears left.

When visiting Grandma Lula, I talked to her asking questions and acting as though she responded to me. One day in doing this, she smiled at me, and I could see that her eyes were teary. I lay in bed with her and just hugged her. I also told her about the baby and that I could not wait for her to see him. Yes, I said "him" because she already had a great-granddaughter, so now she had to have a great-grandson. The months seemed to pass quickly with no change in Grandma Lula's condition.

Learning to Let Go

Jim, Sonya, and I arrived early on a Saturday afternoon in Louisville. When we arrived at Mom and Dad's house on that day, getting ready to go to see Grandma Lula, my mom said she wanted to go with me as Jim took Sonya to spend some time with his sister and her children, who lived about thirty minutes away. I said "great," and off we went. But as we drove to see Grandma, my mom looked at me and said, "Connie, I know that you want Mama to live to see the baby, but have you thought about what your grandma wants?"

I looked at my mom and asked, "What do you mean?"

My mom continued, "Mama had talked with me not long ago about how she felt about living. To her, living was having the ability to do what she liked, eating, drinking, and enjoying her family. Mama is resting comfortably now, but I truly believe she is holding on because you refuse to let go. Ask God to help you to let her go so she can be at peace."

I had to pull the car over as I began to cry. The pain of losing Grandma Lula hurt so bad that I was aching all over. I knew my mom was right and that I had to put aside what I was feeling and be in touch with what Grandma was feeling.

When we arrived at the facility, Mom told me that I could go to see Grandma, and she would wait for me in the car. I understood what she was saying and got myself together for the visit. That day, Grandma looked so pretty as she was wearing a pink gown, her favorite color. She was also looking directly at me with her eyes focused. I told her how beautiful she looked and that I was glad to see her. But I told her, "I know that you love all of us and that you probably miss being with us like we always have been in the past. I really wanted you to be here to see the baby and be a part of his life. But Grandma, I know that you are prepared to leave here to be with Jesus and that I have been selfish. If you are ready to go, then feel free to go. I have your love in my heart and the wisdom that you have shared with me all my life. All of us will see you in heaven. I will always love you!"

I sat on the bed and rested my head on her shoulder like I had done as a little girl while putting my hand on her left hand. We sat there for a while, just being together. After a while, I got up and wished Grandma a good night. The following Saturday, February 21, 1981, Grandma Lula went to be with Jesus. Two days later, Aunt Thelma, Grandma's sister, also went to be with Jesus, causing a double blow to the family because of losing two such loved people so quickly.

Grandma Lula was laid to rest next to her beloved husband, Moses Brown, who left her some thirty-three years before. It gave me peace to know that now she was with him again as she loved him so very much. And I also remembered Grandma Lula saying:

"Life has been created to live. Place your values in God and family and let God guide you on life's choices…"

Grandma Lula had done just that. I joined the rest of the family as we ate dinner celebrating a life well-lived.

Grandma Maybelle

After Grandma Lula's passing, I talked to Grandma Maybelle about all the feelings that I experienced. My grandmas were close to each other and had been since my parents married in 1949. When I finished giving Grandma Maybelle the details, she looked at me and smiled and shared with me, "Baby, Ms. Lula and I often talked about leaving this world to be with King Jesus. Your Grandma was ready when she had the first stroke, but she told me that she knew that you and the baby (meaning Sonya) needed her for a bit longer. That's why she stayed. I have already told the Lord that I want to leave quickly without suffering." Grandma went on to say, "Remember that for most folks:

'They die just like they live.'

'You preach your own funeral in the way you live.'

and

'Take pride in yourself and remember it's a poor frog that don't praise his own pond.'"

I knew that Grandma Maybelle was serious about leaving quickly as this is something she had talked about for many years. She shared that by seeing many of her friends suffer from strokes as well as heart attacks and other ailments, Grandma Maybelle did not want to be a burden to the family. I never really understood why she felt that way, but I understood better after Grandma Lula passed away. I looked at Grandma Maybelle and asked, "What makes the frog poor?" We both started laughing with her never answering my question.

My Last Time with Grandma Maybelle

We continued with the Sunday dinners and fun weekends, with the holidays always being special times. Grandma Lula had been gone for seven years at this time. For the fourth of July, we had dinner at Mom and Dad's house, with Grandma Maybelle attending. We talked about Grandma Lula with Grandma Maybelle, saying that those were good times. But we always had a fun time, with my spending extra time with Grandma Maybelle as I had to leave the day after the fourth to go to work. I took Grandma home, and we spent time together talking about the good old days and with Grandma sharing several stories that she had told me at least a thousand times over the years. It did not matter as I enjoyed her telling the stories, and they brought back fond memories.

As we began to wind down, our bellies full from dinner and our mouths tired from talking, Grandma Maybelle looked at me and said, "Are you tired from being with this old woman?"

I looked at her and said, "No, ma'am—I love being with this old woman!"

She smiled at me and said, "I will miss these times."

I heard what she said and made the decision not to respond as I knew she was serious.

She continued, "Connie, God has been good to me—I ain't leaving now but I will one day. Don't be sad 'cause God gave me a good life."

I told her I understood what she was saying and that I loved her. She also shared with me that Aunt Betty (her sister) was coming for a visit the following week. I told Grandma that I would come by and spend time with them once Aunt Betty came to town. I left Grandma's house feeling that she would go to be with Jesus at any time. I took the time to thank God for her and asked God to help me when it would be her time to leave.

REMEMBERING GRANDMAS' PRECIOUS *Pearls of Wisdom*

A Request That Could Not Be Ignored

Grandma Maybelle had not seen Aunt Betty for a while. Grandma's sons and grandchildren called her Aunt Betty as she had been married and living in Detroit, MI, with Grandma's grandchildren meeting her as children. At some point, she became divorced and moved back to Louisville. I always liked to see her when she visited Grandma as she always dressed very stylishly and smelled so good. I also liked the way she talked, as she sounded so sophisticated. But there is a difference between visiting a town and living in it.

Louisville, GA, was nothing like Detroit, MI, with Aunt Betty not being happy with living in Louisville. She was always moving to some other city that was at least a few hours away from Louisville. Currently, she was living somewhere close to Atlanta, GA. Grandma Maybelle always knew where Aunt Betty was and had asked her to come for a visit. Aunt Betty told Grandma several times that she was coming but never managed to come for a visit. Grandma Maybelle was always direct and to the point, without any patience for lying. Once Aunt Betty lied to Grandma the third time, Grandma Maybelle ended the conversation by saying: "I won't ask you again—I guess you will find the time to come to my funeral once I am dead." Aunt Betty was in Louisville at Grandma's house the next day.

Grandma Maybelle Meets Jesus

When I returned to Atlanta from my trip to New York and Miami, the flight arrived early, allowing me to take an earlier flight to Augusta. I called Jim to tell him I would be coming home on the earlier flight. He told me that he would meet me at the airport. I told him that would be nice as we could have some time together before driving to my mom and dad's home. He agreed. When I arrived at the airport in Augusta, I saw Jim, and I could tell by the expression on his face that something was wrong. He met me, hugged me, and asked me to sit down for a minute. I did, and he said, "Babe, I hate to tell you this, but Grandma Maybelle passed away two days ago." The news hit me like a rock. When I was able to talk, I asked him what had happened. He then shared with me what happened.

It was the second week of July, with Aunt Betty being on her fourth day visiting with Grandma, with the two of them having a good time. Though Grandma always had prepared food in the freezer, she enjoyed cooking food from scratch for her family and anyone in the neighborhood who was hungry. Grandma had asked Aunt Betty what she wanted for dinner, and Aunt Betty had asked for collard greens, cornbread, fried chicken, and sweet potato pies. Grandma went into the kitchen, put the collard greens on, and took the chicken out of the freezer to thaw. She decided that she would comb her hair and asked Aunt Betty to get the hair oil she used that was on the mantle. Aunt Betty had the oil in her hand ready to give to Grandma Maybelle and had asked Grandma a question. When Grandma did not respond to the question with an answer, Aunt Betty turned around to notice that Grandma was slumped on the sofa. She ran to Grandma and asked what was wrong with no response from Grandma. Aunt Betty told Grandma that she would call the doctor. Grandma looked at her and said, "Don't do that; I am just fine." Grandma was in the arms of Jesus just like she wanted.

The ride to my mom and dad's house was a ride of silence as my mind became flooded with my last visit with Grandma Maybelle. She shared with me her heart during that previous visit so that I could begin to prepare myself for her leaving. I could see this clearly and knew that I had to accept it.

After the funeral service, I took a few extra minutes to stand at Grandma's final resting place. She lived seven years after Grandma Lula's passing, and I did cherish every day with her. It was also strange that I remembered something that she said to me when we attended her youngest son, Fred, Jr.'s funeral in 1980. As she stood at Uncle Fred's gravesite, Grandma Maybelle said:

> "The child you do the most for will do the least for you—but you love all your children so it don't matter—especially after they are no longer with you."

I could not understand why I remembered that saying, but I did. But I also remembered something a lot more important, and that was Grandma saying:

"Be mindful of how you live your life so that when Jesus calls you home, you are ready."

I genuinely believe that Grandma Maybelle was ready, and that thought gave me a feeling of peace!

REMEMBERING THE GOOD TIMES WITH MY GRANDMAS

With both of my grandmas gone, life looked a lot different. I had depended on these incredible women for so much. They talked to me, shared so many beautiful stories about their lives, and kept me ever mindful of the importance of being a godly woman, wife, and mother. Each of them also reminded me that one day with God's grace and wisdom, I would be a grandma and that I should live a life that is pleasing to God and my family

CHAPTER 5
DEALING WITH LIFE'S HARD BLOWS

Betrayal

I was incredibly happy in my marriage; however, I could see some changes taking place that I did not think were good. Being a flight attendant had improved over the years, with my working an average of ten to eleven days a month. Attending the different activities that Sonya and Karic had in school was so much fun reminding me of my younger days. My parents were also present at these activities, reminding me of the joy they had when attending my activities. But I noticed that Jim was becoming distant while also needing to work when the children had activities in school. He also acted as though he had something on his mind that he did not know how to share. We had always talked to each other about everything, so I just believed that this was yet another phase our marriage would go through with us coming out better after the test. But I was very wrong.

Being raised in an atmosphere where honesty is expected and valued, accepting the signs of betrayal is challenging. Even worse is recognizing the signs when you have married someone you love and who has said they love you too. I took my marriage vows seriously; therefore, I was not looking for a way out of the marriage but ways to continue to make it work. Another critical thing to me was to be "happily" married, not just stay with my husband for the sake of being together. To succeed, marriage must have both people in love and working together. My parents did this and were successful, and so did my grandmas; hence, the reason that I desired to be married in the first place. I prayed to God to show me what to do as I was experiencing feelings that I had never experienced before. My heart ached, and I could not make it stop. Work became a form of refuge as it took my mind off my troubles in my marriage, allowing me to focus on the passengers and their needs. But the minute the plane landed on the last leg of a trip; reality set in with my having to wonder what sad news would be waiting on me when I arrived home. The only joy of coming home from work was seeing my children and my parents; after that, there was no other joy—just the feeling of emptiness.

Growing Apart

Sometimes couples ignore that they are growing apart. Like most married people, I focused on my family and work and ensuring that the children's needs were met. I assumed that Jim felt the same way; however, I was wrong. But whether I accepted the truth or not, the reality was that Jim was no longer paying attention to us and was not making any type of investment into the marriage and the relationship that two people have when married. Trust was also slipping away with doubt and fear creeping in. Once lies are discovered and excuses are continually made, trust is broken down. While I had no idea what was causing this change, it really did not matter. This was a type of covert betrayal that kept getting worse.

I wanted my marriage to work, so I kept making attempts to talk to Jim. Finally, one afternoon I told Jim that I wanted our marriage to be the way it used to be. Jim told me he was tired of working so hard with my making more money and working fewer hours. I looked at him in disbelief and said, "So let me make sure I am hearing you right. You are upset because I make more money than you do?"

He said, "All that I am saying is I just need a break."

I responded, "When you have a family, you don't have time for breaks. We have children who need food, clothes and have other needs. There is also the private school tuition and the transportation costs for them to attend school. If you want to change careers, I have no problem with that, as you have been supportive of my choices. But working is something that you will have to do at least until the children are adults."

Jim just got up, looked at me disgustedly, got in the car, and left. I could not believe it. I was utterly devastated and cried myself to sleep that night. But I also remembered Grandma Lula's saying:

> *"Know the difference between making a choice and making a mistake."*

I realized that Jim had made a choice to make an excuse for no longer desiring to work. This was an example of irresponsibility without reason. My thoughts also went to the word of God concerning Jesus' betrayal by Judas (John 18:5). This is a hurt that cannot be described adequately in words, as reading about betrayal is one thing, but experiencing it is totally different!

The Downward Spiral

After our disagreement, many others followed, making it exceedingly difficult to have a conversation that did not lead to an argument. Since arguments were not part of my DNA, I stopped initiating conversations and began considering separating from Jim. I remembered Grandma Maybelle saying:

> *"Don't make decisions when you get mad because you will regret them."*

I was outraged, so I let the separation idea go. Our conversations became fewer, with Jim avoiding me and my not desiring to be with him. I had to realize that something else was going on that was bringing about this change. Maybe Christian counseling would help. I suggested this idea to Jim with him rejecting the idea immediately. I told him I was open to his suggestions, and he said he did not have any suggestions. In a moment, I remembered what Grandma Lula said:

> *"Never choose to overlook the truth even when you don't want to accept it."*

Something was happening with Jim, and if changes did not occur soon, our marriage would be destroyed with our children experiencing behavioral problems because of all of the arguing. Their future would be potentially jeopardized because of the negative actions of their parents. The time for crying was over for me with my going to Christian counseling to devise a plan that I hoped would improve our present situation.

Guidance with Godly Advice

Being from a small town has advantages and disadvantages, with the most prominent disadvantage being people assuming that they know your business as though it were their own while also talking about your business even though they know nothing. I went for Christian counseling but not in Louisville. I went to a church that I attended in Los Angeles, CA, that I could go to on a layover. I knew that since I was not known personally, the advice would be more directed based on what was occurring in my life. When I shared what was happening, the counselor let me know that both Jim and I needed counseling and that she believed other things were occurring that I had no knowledge about. The counselor and I prayed together before I left, feeling confident in God revealing what needed to be done in this situation and following that guidance. Grandma Lula used to say:

> "Prayer is not just about talking to God but about listening to what God tells you."

When I returned home from that trip, Jim came home. I shared with Jim that I believed we needed to go to counseling so that we could work through whatever issues were occurring. He answered me by saying that he was not going to counseling for any reason and that I was the one with the problem. At this point, I realized Jim and I were no longer on the same page when it came to not only marriage but our lives overall. I told Jim that if he did not want to get counseling, then perhaps we needed to separate so that he could determine what was of importance to him. He said this was not a problem for him and proceeded to get in the car and leave. Since he left without taking any other clothes with him, I assumed he thought that I was joking. I decided to pack his clothes and had them waiting upon his return. Three days later, around 7 p.m., Jim returned, finding locks changed and his clothes nicely packed and waiting for him underneath the garage. Though my heart was broken, I knew that I had made the best decision. We were no longer compatible, and Jim did not desire to work with me to make needed changes.

The Twenty-Year Mark

I do not know if there is anything special about twenty years, but this was definitely what I call a milestone year in my life. After separating from Jim, I took the advice of a counselor and talked with a lawyer. Since I had two children, I wanted to ensure that I looked out for them. The lawyer advised me to have divorce papers served on Jim as quickly as possible. I had told the lawyer that I did not want a divorce; however, the lawyer informed me that this was not about what I wanted but that Jim was doing things that usually involved the practice of unethical behavior. This was another one of those situations where I knew the lawyer was telling the truth even though I did not want to believe it. The lawyer also said that if things worked out between Jim and me, then great, but if not, Jim would be served with divorce papers while we had some knowledge of his location. I agreed with the lawyer: Jim was served with the divorce papers in less than two weeks. I also remembered that Grandma Maybelle said:

> *"Don't ever fail to take advice from someone you know is giving it! Being a fool is bad but being a fool on purpose is downright ignorant."*

Having to Break the News to the Children

No one in love desires to be separated but worse than the separation was having to share the news with the children. Sonya was a teenager who had a strong connection with her dad. She was incredibly sad when I shared that the four of us would no longer live together for a while. She cried a little but said she hoped her dad would be okay. Karic was much younger, only six, with Jim not really spending that much time with him. Undoubtedly, Karic was not really that emotional about the situation. I think that it was at this point that I realized Jim had not only ignored me but had also ignored his son most of all. I truly realized that I had made the right decision, even though it was painful. Telling my mom and dad was not difficult as they believed I should have separated earlier. One thing I loved about my parents was that they never involved themselves in my marriage but always let me know they were there if needed. It was through their love and support that I was able to make this difficult choice.

Working on ME

During the separation, I began looking at myself and determining what I needed to do to improve myself. My entire adult life had been wrapped around Jim, our marriage, and the children. Now I had to work on improving myself while being a single parent. Since I had always had the support of my parents, I never felt alone. There was also my uncle who lived next to us, so I knew that not only would I be fine, but that my children would also have support while making the adjustment to their father not being present.

I continued Christian counseling on my own to discover what I did wrong or had possibly overlooked in my marriage. There was a lot of disappointment for me as my parents and grandparents had successful marriages even through challenging times. In the counseling sessions, I mentioned this disappointment with the counselor allowing me to share my innermost feelings. Maybe I did not focus on my marriage as much as I should have focused on it. Could I have been a better wife? Is it possible that I ignored Jim? The questions and excuses were endless. The counselor simply listened, allowing me to talk out loud. Finally, I realized that no matter what I thought, Jim could have shared with me anything that he felt needed changing so that we could work on it *together*. Marriage takes both people working together, not just one. And I also knew that God had nothing to do with the failure of the marriage as God is all about success. Grandma Lula once said:

> *"God will only act in your life if you let Him, and always remember that God does not force anybody to do anything. Free will is something we all have that causes us problems sometimes."*

Within six months, I was more in touch with myself and better understood what I wanted to do with my life. My first focus was on building a better relationship with Jesus, thereby spending time reading the Bible and focusing on being my best self. Recalling an earlier promise I made to God when my daughter was born, my second focus was being the best mother that I could be to my children. I enjoyed being a mother very much and counted every moment with my children as a moment of a great investment.

Two years passed very quickly with my learning more about my children and becoming even more involved in their activities. Sonya had a tutor helping her improve in mathematics and science, and Karic played sports while taking karate. I became an International Coordinator so that I could earn more income while having more time off to be with my children. The lawyer was right with my remembering that Grandma Lula had said:

> *"Marriage brings with it many troubles—spend time in prayer and make sure you hear from God before doing it."*

I knew it was time to get the divorce that I did not desire to get, but since I had not heard from Jim in two years, it was time to move forward as he had not thought about the children or me. The divorce was finalized that August, which was a little short of twenty years of marriage. My lawyer took me out to lunch and walked the papers over to the courthouse to be filed. He said, "Now you can move forward with your life, and I know it will be a good one." WOW—a nineteen-year and ten-month marriage had ended, and I could not prevent it from ending! It was a challenge not to feel like a failure, yet I knew I had done all I could.

Changes within the Airline Industry

Not only were changes taking place in my personal life, but changes were also taking place at work. The airline that had always made money was now experiencing changes that were outside of its control. Deregulation was taking place, bringing about changes within the airline industry that had to be reckoned with. The airline was also known as a top airline paying top salaries to all its employees, which was now seen as a cause for many of its financial woes.

I had to inform the airline of my pending divorce and the finalizing of that divorce. However, as the airline began to make changes, people who had enough seniority to retire started to retire, with my supervisor telling me she would retire in one month. I was devastated at the news and decided to change bases, moving from the Atlanta hub to the Los Angeles hub and, finally, the Portland hub. This was yet another one of those "divine decisions" as the airline began devising a plan to remove people with fifteen years or more of service under questionable circumstances. Ultimately, I was "laid off" just one month short of twenty years. At the time, this seemed like the end of my life; however, God had a better plan granting me more than I could have thought possible. Grandma Lula was right when she said:

"God's plan is the best plan even when you don't understand."

I trusted God to guide me with the rest of my life and the many challenges that I knew would occur. He is doing just that, and I will share that good news in Book II.

In my grandmas' absence, one good thing was that neither of them was aware of my divorce from the man I believed would love me forever. The tragedy was that I could no longer talk to them about all the many issues that arose that led to the failure of my marriage. And yet, it was the remembrance of their wisdom and godly advice that enabled me to make one of the hardest decisions that I had ever made in my life. For that, I am still grateful even today.

CHAPTER 6
WHAT NOW?

One of the beautiful things about life is that it continuously changes while also remaining the same. As I look at my life, my grandmas played a significant role in my successes, and I also benefited from their wisdom when experiencing the many challenges associated with living. But there are many differences between my life with my grandmas and me as a grandma.

LIFE IS VIEWED DIFFERENTLY TODAY

When I was a child, it was easy to know right from wrong, with the majority of people doing their best to live right. People made mistakes; however, they knew it was better to admit the mistake, apologize, move on, and not repeat it. This right living involved being truthful and honest and making it a practice at home and work.

Today in our society, people have no problem emphasizing what they choose to do while also making excuses for not doing what is right. There are even court shows for these people, including "Couples Court," where people appear before a married couple who are judges and have been married for over thirty years, practicing faithfulness, honesty, and effective communication. Most of the couples appearing on the show live together without being legally married and have children within the relationship. They appear on the show because they believe that the person with whom they are living is being unfaithful.

But what is amazing is that even when it is proven that one or the other partner is cheating, many decide to try to work things out even though no commitment has been made. Some couples return to the show for a second time. This is at best puzzling to me as I was legally married, having to become divorced when my husband decided that he no longer desired to be married. Was it painful? Yes. Did I hate that this was happening? Yes. But what is to be gained in staying in a relationship without each person being committed? To me, it is easy to see that if a person can practice infidelity in a relationship without having to be accountable for their actions, this will continue forever. One thing that Grandma Maybelle said over and over again was:

> "Have respect for yourself 'cause people will only treat you as good as you treat yourself."

What I Was Exposed to as a Child

My parents had control of what I saw on television, the people with whom I associated, and also knew exactly where I was located at all times. When I became a teenager, there were curfews with my not being allowed to go one minute over that set time. Our television had only three channels with three networks, including ABC, NBC, and CBS. Family programming allowed family shows such as *Bonanza*, *The Rifleman*, *Father Knows Best*, and *Leave It to Beaver*. These shows revealed the importance of family and how families loved and respected each other. There was always some type of challenge with the mother and father approaching the children with correction.

But most importantly, there was always a moral to the story teaching those watching the importance of love, faith, and honesty. I watched no television after 9 p.m. as this was bedtime when I was young. Once in high school, there was truly little time for television as my homework took up much of my time, even on the weekends.

As an adolescent, teaching relative to sex emphasized marriage and the family and the importance of the marriage coming *before* the family. People were also unashamed to talk about the Bible, the importance of attending church, and the need to live in a manner that set an example for anyone who might consider deviating from living in this manner.

I only became exposed to negatives such as racism when I was transferred from a predominately Black school to a white school. There were news reports about the civil rights movement and the brutality of the police toward people of color; however, this seemed like something far away from my little hometown. And even amid this chaos at my new school, once a few white students realized that Black students differed only because of having darker skin, the Black and white students started to come together with understanding, with some of us becoming friends.

When I moved to Atlanta, GA, to attend dental school, I discovered that people had no problem lying, cheating, stealing, being dishonest, and being evil to others just because they could. But through the combination of my parents always allowing me to talk about any issues that I may have, my grandmother's sharing their wisdom concerning how life should be lived, and my dependence on God, I learned to avoid and disassociate with those whom I knew practiced dishonesty while also making up my mind not to become negative while being around unethical people.

Raising My Children

My children were raised very similarly to how I was raised, even though they were exposed to much more at a much earlier age. Sex education was a part of the middle school and high school curriculum with books that gave precise illustrations. When I asked my mother about the menstrual cycle, she gave me a pamphlet to read and told me to ask her any questions if I did not understand. Though I did not really understand, I could tell that my mother did not really want to talk about this subject; so, I moved on. When my daughter asked me what it meant to have a cycle, I explained the process to her in detail, and she was good to go. After attending a class on sex education, Sonya shared what she had learned, giving me greater confidence for the next set of questions I knew she would ask.

When it came to sharing the wisdom that my grandmothers had shared with me, my son and daughter listened but not in the same manner that I did. When I would begin to share a story, my son would say, "Oh Lord, here comes another story." Yet, he would listen attentively, and so would Sonya. I also learned later that he has shared these same stories with his wife and children in great detail. Each of my children respects me as their mother and has been obedient even when disagreeing with some of the things that I shared. Yes, there were the teenage years with each of them having some issues, but what child does not have problems at this stage in their lives? What is of importance is that I could stay in touch with them even during changing times with them speaking with me weekly when they left home. They still talk to me weekly now, which means more to me because we talk about them and my grandchildren.

The Wisdom That I Offer as a Grandma

My grandchildren were more intelligent at three years than I was at twelve. Seeing my two-year-old grandson operate his mother's cell phone to view his cartoons, my five-year-old grandson asking his football coach if he had a girlfriend because he (my grandson) had never seen him with one, and my ten-year-old granddaughter sharing how her teacher seemed to experience a gap when teaching a specific subject in class brought me to the reality of how much my grandchildren are in touch with what is going on in the world. And while these are only a few of the many examples that I can offer, I can promise you that I cannot be vague when explaining anything to my grandchildren, who range in age now between twenty-three years and two years. They have tablets and use computers in the classroom and at home. They know about international countries, different languages, and social media. This is a generation that has knowledge at their fingertips; however, they need guidance from their parents and grandparents so that they know the difference between right and wrong and use that knowledge when making decisions that will impact their lives in the present and future.

My Sayings

My sayings are somewhat similar to my grandma's sayings but are relevant to today and sound like this:

When helping my granddaughter with her homework:

"Alexa OFF! Learn how to use your brain versus Alexa as you need to learn how to think."

In general conversation about life and school:

"Place value on telling the truth as it is one thing that never changes."

WHAT NOW?

"Quit trying to fit in with people—everyone is not your friend."

"Truth doesn't have a version."

"Spare me the excuses of why you didn't do what was expected—just do it."

"You have one major task as a child and that is to pay attention and learn what is being taught."

"You are not expected to understand some things; hence, the reason for having parents and grandparents."

"No matter what society may tell you, God is real and does exist and the Bible is the final authority on every issue in life."

"A lot can be learned by reading and writing—make these two tasks a priority in your life."

"Life is a gift—don't waste it using drugs. You will need your brain to be in full operation for the rest of your life."

"When in doubt ask questions. If the answer you receive doesn't make sense, ask someone you know you can trust."

"As a woman, take pride in dressing with class. No man needs to be able to see your entire body at a glance."

"Don't be ashamed of the Gospel of Jesus Christ as being a Christian pays far more than it costs."

While this is only a shortlist, I am sure that I will have more sayings as my grandchildren grow up asking more questions. The best thing that I can offer my grandchildren is to live a life that exemplifies what I tell them.

Today, we live in a society that lacks a moral compass, with people feeling free to do anything and everything they want to do. I make no judgments and realize that all of us make mistakes; however, it is of importance to realize that what my grandma said is still true:

Remembering Grandmas' Precious *Pearls of Wisdom*

"You will reap what you sow, so be careful of what you do as it will come back to you."

It is still essential to be honest, truthful, and do what is right even when no one is looking. We all have made mistakes and will make more; however, it is also important to acknowledge those mistakes, ask for forgiveness, and purpose in your heart not to make the same mistake again. Life does bring with it challenges that can seem insurmountable; and even when doing right, sometimes adversity comes, but we must keep in mind that no matter what we may think or feel, in the end, we must be able to look in the mirror and be pleased with what we see. It took years for me to understand that success is not measured by a career, the amount of money in the bank, or by how many people like us. True success is measured by how we live our lives daily having faith in Jesus Christ while helping and loving others, especially family. This is what my parents and grandmas did without having a second thought. As for me, I will forever be thankful for this life that I have been given and will continue living it to the fullest while keeping in mind and leaning on the sayings of my grandmas that I see as my grandmas' precious pearls of wisdom!

CPSIA information can be obtained
at www.ICGtesting.com
Printed in the USA
BVHW051939200423
662743BV00012B/213